THE
CIVIL
WAR

THE
CIVIL
WAR

A Concise Military History
of the War Between the States
1861-1865

Adapted from *American Military History*
Office of the Chief of Military History
United States Army

Maurice Matloff
General Editor

Illustrated by John W. Howard

DAVID McKAY COMPANY, INC.
New York

Adapted from *American Military History*
Office of the Chief of Military History
United States Army

Maurice Matloff, General Editor

Published by
David McKay Company, Inc.
750 Third Avenue
New York, New York 10017

Library of Congress Cataloging in Publication Data
Main entry under title:

The Civil War.

Includes index.
1. United States—History—Civil War, 1861-1865—
Campaigns and battles. I. Matloff, Maurice, 1915-
II. Matloff, Maurice, 1915-   American military
history. III. Title.
E470.C55   973.7′3   77-18796
ISBN 0-679-50840-6

Portraits from Picture Collection,
The Branch Libraries, The New York Public Library

10-9-8-7-6-5-4-3

CONTENTS

THE
CIVIL
WAR

CHAPTER 1
1861

North and South were on a collision course.

During the administration of President James Buchanan, 1857–61, tensions over the issue of extending slavery into the western territories mounted alarmingly. Events were rushing the nation toward disunion, even war. Along with slavery, the shifting social, economic, political, and constitutional problems of the fast-growing country fragmented its citizenry. After open warfare broke out in Kansas Territory among slaveholders, abolitionists, and opportunists, the battle lines of opinion hardened. President Buchanan quieted Kansas by using the Regular Army, but the army was too small and too scattered to suppress the struggles that were almost certain to break out in the border states.

In 1859 John Brown, who had won notoriety in "Bleeding Kansas," seized the Federal arsenal at Harpers Ferry in a mad attempt to foment a slave uprising within a slaveholding state. Federal troops were called on to suppress the new outbreak, and pressures and emotions rose on the eve of the 1860 elections. Republican Abraham Lincoln was elected to succeed Buchanan; although he failed to win a majority of the popular vote, he received 180 of the 303 electoral votes. His inauguration would take place March 4, 1861. During this lame-duck period, Mr. Buchanan was unable to control events and the country continued to lose cohesion.

ABRAHAM LINCOLN

Secession, Sumter, and Standing to Arms

Abraham Lincoln's election to the Presidency on November 6, 1860, triggered South Carolina on December 20 to enact an ordinance declaring "the union now subsisting between South Carolina and other States, under the name of the 'United States of America,' is hereby dissolved." Within six weeks, six other deep-South states seceded from the Union and seized Federal property inside their borders, including military installations, save for Fort Pickens outside Pensacola and Fort Sumter in Charleston Harbor. *(Map 1)* To the seven states that formed the Confederate States of America on February 18, 1861, at Montgomery, Alabama, retention of the forts by the U.S. Government was equivalent to a warlike act. To provide his fledgling government with a military force, on March 6 the new Confederate Executive, Jefferson Davis, called for a 100,000-man volunteer force to serve for twelve months.

The creation of a rival War Department south of the 35th parallel shattered the composition of the Regular Army and disrupted its activities, particularly in Texas, where Maj. Gen. David E. Twiggs surrendered his entire command. With an actual strength of 1,080 officers and 14,926 enlisted men on June 30, 1860, the Regular Army was based on 5-year enlistments. Recruited heavily from men of foreign birth, the United States Army consisted of ten regiments of infantry, four of artillery, two of cavalry, two of dragoons, and one of mounted riflemen. It was not a unified striking force. The Regular Army was deployed within seven departments, six of them west of the Mississippi. Of 198 line companies, 183 were scattered in 79 isolated posts in the territories. The remaining 15 were in garrisons along the Canadian border and on the Atlantic coast.

Created by Secretary of War John C. Calhoun and expanded by Secretary of War Davis in 1853, the departments of the United States Army had become powerful institutions by the eve of the Civil War. Within each of the trans-Mississippi departments a senior colonel or general officer by brevet commanded some 2,000 officers and men. All the states east of the Mississippi constituted the Department of the East, where Bvt. Maj. Gen. John E. Wool controlled 929 Regulars. A department commander was responsible for mobilizing and training militia and volunteer forces called into Federal service, and for co-ordinating his resources with any expeditionary force commander who operated inside his territory or crossed through his department. A department commander often doubled in command. He was responsible for the administration of his

3

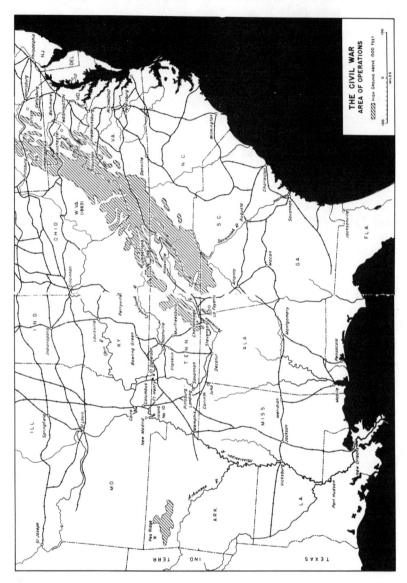

Map 1

department as well as for conduct of operations in the field. He often had a dual staff arrangement, one departmental and another for the campaign. For strategic guidance and major decisions he looked to the President and General in Chief; for administrative support he channeled his requirements through the Secretary of War to the appropriate bureau chief. In the modern sense he had no corps of staff experts who could assist him in equating his strategic goals with his logistical needs. In many respects the departmental system was a major reason why the Union armies during the Civil War operated like a team of balky horses.

The 1,676 numbered paragraphs of the U.S. Army Regulations governed the actions of a department commander. The provisions concerning Army organization and tactics were archaic in most cases despite Davis' efforts in 1857 to update the Regulations to reflect the experience of the Mexican War. During the Civil War, the Regulations would be slightly modified to incorporate the military laws passed by two wartime Congresses. In the South these same Regulations would govern the policy and procedures of the Confederate forces.

The roster of the Regular Army was altered considerably by Davis' action in creating a Confederate Army. Of the active officer corps numbering 1,080, 286 resigned or were dismissed and entered the Confederate service. (At least 26 enlisted men are known to have violated their oaths.) West Point graduates on the active list numbered 824; of these, 184 were among the officers who offered their swords to the Confederacy. Of the approximately 900 graduates then in civil life, 114 returned to the Union Army and 99 others sought southern commissions. General in Chief Scott and Col. George H. Thomas of Virginia were southerners who fought for the Union. More serious than their numbers, however, was the high caliber of the officers who joined the Confederacy; many were regimental commanders and three had commanded at departmental level.

With military preparations under way, Davis dispatched commissioners to Washington a few days after Lincoln's inauguration on March 4, 1861, to treat for the speedy takeover of Forts Sumter and Pickens. Informally reassured that the forts would not be provisioned without proper notice, the envoys returned to

5

JEFFERSON DAVIS

Montgomery expecting an uneventful evacuation of Sumter.
President Lincoln had to move cautiously, for he knew Sumter's
supplies were giving out. As each March day passed, Sumter ag-
gravated the harshness of Lincoln's dilemma. In case of war, the
fort had no strategic value. If Lincoln reinforced it, Davis would

have his act of provocation and Lincoln might drive eight more slaveholding states out of the Union. If Sumter was not succored, the North might cool its enthusiasm for the Union concept and become accustomed to having a confederation south of the Mason-Dixon line.

President Lincoln spent a fortnight listening to the conflicting counsel of his constitutional advisers, and made up his own mind on March 29 to resupply Fort Sumter with provisions only. No effort would be made to increase its military power. By sea he soon dispatched a token expedition and on April 8 notified South Carolina's governor of his decision. The next move was up to the local Confederate commander, Brig. Gen. Pierre G. T. Beauregard. On the 11th, Maj. Robert Anderson, Sumter's commander, politely but firmly rejected a formal surrender demand. At 4:30 the next morning Confederate batteries began a 34-hour bombardment. Anderson's 90-man garrison returned it in earnest, but Sumter's guns were no match for the concentric fire from Confederate artillery. Offered honorable terms on April 14 Anderson surrendered the Federal fort, saluted his U.S. flag with fifty guns, and, with his command, was conveyed to the fleet outside the harbor to be taken to New York City.

The Confederates had fired the first shot of the war, and with that act removed many difficulties from Lincoln's path to preserve the Union. On the 15th Lincoln personally penned a proclamation declaring the seven southern states in insurrection against the laws of the United States. To strangle the Confederacy, on the 19th Lincoln declared the entire coast from South Carolina to Texas under naval blockade. To augment the reduced Regular Army, Lincoln asked the governors of the loyal states for 75,000 militiamen to serve for three months, the maximum time permissible under existing laws. With a unanimity which astonished most people, the northern states responded with 100,000 men. Within the eight slave states still in the Union, the militia call to suppress the rebellion was angrily and promptly rejected, and the President's decision to coerce the Confederacy moved Virginia, North Carolina, Tennessee, and Arkansas to join it.

As spring changed into summer the magnitude of the job that

GENERAL ROBERT E. LEE

the Union had proclaimed for itself—the conquest of an area the size of western Europe, save Scandinavia and Italy, defended by a plucky and proud people and favored by military geography—was imperfectly understood. Although Lincoln later emerged as a diligent student of warfare, he was as yet unversed in the art.

His rival, Davis, from the outset knew his military men quite well and thoroughly understood the mechanics of building a fighting force. Yet, as time passed, Davis was to mismanage his government and its military affairs more and more.

Virginia's secession caused Col. Robert E. Lee, Scott's choice to be the Union's field leader, to resign his commission and offer his services to his state. The Confederates moved their capital to Richmond, Virginia, site of the largest iron works in the south and one hundred miles south of the Union capital, Washington. On May 23, Union forces crossed into northern Virginia, occupying Arlington Heights and Alexandria. With Virginia and North Carolina in rebellion, Lincoln extended the naval blockade and called for a large volunteer army backed by an increased Regular force.

Correctly anticipating that Congress in its session to open July 4 would approve his actions, Lincoln, on his own authority, established 40 regiments of U.S. Volunteers (42,034 men) to serve three years or for the duration of the war. He ordered the Regular Army increased by one regiment of artillery, one of cavalry, and eight of infantry (actually, nine regiments were added), or 22,714 men, and the Navy by 18,000 sailors. The new Regular infantry regiments were each to have three battalions of about 800 men, in contrast to the one-battalion structure in the existing Regular and volunteer regiments. Because the recruits preferred the larger bonuses, laxer discipline, and easy-going atmosphere of the volunteers, most of the newly constituted regiments were never able to fill their additional battalions to authorized strength.

The enthusiastic response to Lincoln's various calls had forced him to ask the governors to scale down the induction of men. The overtaxed camps could not handle the increased manpower. In raising the Army Lincoln used methods that dated back to Washington's day. The combat efficiency and state of training of the new units varied from good to very poor. Some militia regiments were well trained and equipped, others were regiments in name only. The soldiers often elected their own company officers, and the governors commissioned majors and colonels. The President appointed generals. Although many of the newly commissioned officers proved to be enthusiastic,

9

devoted to duty, and eager to learn, incompetents were also appointed. Before the end of 1861, however, officers were being required to prove their qualifications before examining boards; those found unfit were allowed to resign.

Frequently advised by governors and congressmen, Lincoln selected generals from among leading politicians in order to give himself a broader base of political support. Some political generals, such as John A. Logan and Francis P. Blair, Jr., distinguished themselves, whereas others proved military hindrances. Lincoln gave a majority of the commissions in the first forty volunteer units to Regulars on active duty, to former West Pointers like George B. McClellan who had resigned to pursue a business career, or to those who had held volunteer commissions during the Mexican War. On the other hand, Davis never gave higher than a brigade command to a Confederate volunteer officer until he had proved himself in battle.

Both North and South failed to develop a good system of replacement of individuals in volunteer units. The Confederacy, though hamstrung by its insistence that Texans be commanded by Texans and Georgians by Georgians and by governors' demands for retaining home guards, did devise a regimental system that stood up well until the closing days of the war. Except for Wisconsin, Illinois, and Vermont, the Union armies never had an efficient volunteer replacement system. As battle losses mounted and the ranks of veteran regiments thinned, commanders were forced to send men back to their home states on recruiting duty or face the disbandment of their regiments. Northern governors with patronage in mind preferred to raise new regiments, allowing battle-tested ones to decline to company proportions.

The enlisted Regular Army was kept intact for the duration of the war. Many critics believed that the Regulars should have been used to cadre the volunteer units. But this practice was initially impossible during the summer of 1861 for at least two reasons: Lincoln did not foresee a long war, and the majority of Regulars were needed on the frontier until trained men could replace them. In addition, Lincoln's critics overlooked the breakdown in morale that would have accompanied the breakup of old line regiments, many of which had histories and honors dating back to the War of 1812. An officer holding a Regular commission in 1861 had to resign to accept a commission in the volunteers unless the War Department specifically released him. Most Regulars were loath to resign, uncertain that they would be recalled to active duty after the war. Thus, during 1861 and part of 1862, promotion in the Regular Army was slow. All Regulars could accept commissions in the volunteers by 1862, and in many cases the year that they had spent in small unit command seasoning had its reward in advancing them to higher commands. Ulysses S. Grant and William T. Sherman, both U.S. Military Academy graduates returning from civilian life, asked specifically for volunteer regimental commands at first and soon advanced rapidly to general officer posts.

The Opponents

As North and South lined up for battle, clearly the preponderance of productive capacity, manpower, and agricultural potential lay on the side of the North. Its crops were worth more annually than those of the South, which had concentrated on growing cotton, tobacco, and rice. Between February and May 1861 the Confederate authorities missed the opportunity of shipping baled cotton to England and drawing bills against it for the purchase of arms. In seapower, railroads, material wealth, and industrial capacity to produce iron and munitions the North was vastly superior to the South. This disparity became even more pronounced as the ever-tightening blockade gradually cut off the Confederacy from foreign imports. The North had more mules and horses, a logistical advantage of great importance since supplies had to be carried to the troops from rail and river heads.

According to the census of 1860 the population of the United States numbered 31,443,321 persons. Approximately 23,000,000 of them were in the twenty-two northern states and 9,000,000 in the eleven states that later seceded. Of the latter total, 3,500,000 were slaves. The size of the opposing armies would reflect this disparity. At one time or another about 2,100,000 men would

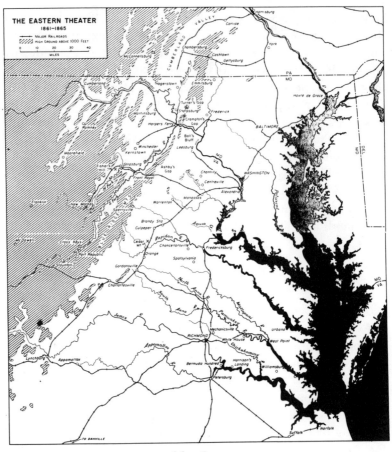

Map 2

serve in the northern armies, while some 800,000 to 900,000 men would serve the South. Peak strength of the two forces would be about 1,000,000 and 600,000, respectively.

Not all the advantages lay with the North. The South possessed good interior lines of communications, and its 3,550-mile coast line, embracing 189 harbors and navigable river mouths, was difficult to blockade effectively. Possessors of a rich military record in wars against the British, Spanish, Mexicans, and Indians, the southerners initially managed to form excellent cavalry units more easily than the North and used them with considerable ·skill against the invading infantry. As the war moved along, the armies on both sides demonstrated high degrees of military skill and bravery. Man for man they became almost evenly matched, and their battles were among the bloodiest in modern history.

Jefferson Davis hoped that the sympathy or even intervention of European powers might more than compensate for the Confederacy's lack of material resources. This hope, largely illusory from the start, became less and less likely of realization with the emancipation of the slaves, with every Union victory, and with the increasing effectiveness of the blockade.

Militarily, the South's greatest advantage over the North was simply the fact that if not attacked it could win by doing nothing. To restore the Union Federal forces would have to conquer the Confederacy. Thus the arena of action lay below the strategic line of the Potomac and Ohio Rivers. Here geography divided the theater of war into three interrelated theaters of operations. The eastern theater lay between the Atlantic Ocean and the Appalachian Mountains; the western theater embraced the area from the Appalachians to the Mississippi; and the trans-Mississippi theater ran westward to the Pacific Ocean. *(Map 2)*

In the east, the strategic triangle of northern Virginia shielded invasion routes. Its apex aimed arrowlike at the Federal capital; the Potomac River and the lower Chesapeake Bay formed its right leg; its left bounded on the Blue Ridge and the adjacent Shenandoah Valley; and the base of the triangle followed the basin of the James and Appomattox Rivers. Richmond stood halfway between the bay and the valley. For three and a half years Federal commanders would be defeated on the legs and in the center of this triangle as they tried to take Richmond and defeat the Army of Northern Virginia under Lee. In three neighboring counties within this triangle more than half a million men would clash in mortal combat; more would die in these counties than in the Revolutionary War, the War of 1812, the War with Mexico, and all the Indian wars combined. To bring the Confederates out of this triangle the North would have to execute an operation aimed at breaking through the base line along the James and Appomattox Rivers.

The hammer for swinging against the anvil of Virginia came from the line of the Ohio River as Union forces moved along the

13

invasion routes of the Green, Cumberland, Tennessee, and Mississippi Rivers. To breach the lower reaches of the Appalachians, the Federals needed the railroad centers at Nashville, Chattanooga, and Atlanta; with them they could strike northward through the Carolinas toward the line of the James. But in the spring of 1861, the anvil and hammer concept had not yet occurred to the military leaders in Washington. Only the General in Chief, Winfield Scott, had a concrete strategic proposal for waging total war. He recommended to Lincoln that time be taken to train an army of 85,000 men and that the naval blockade of the Confederacy be enforced. Then the Army was to advance down the Mississippi to divide and conquer the South. The press ridiculed the strategy, calling it the Anaconda Plan. But few leaders examined the South in terms of its military geography or concentrated on a strategy to prevail over it. Instead, most thought in terms of political boundaries and a short war that would end with the capture of Richmond.

Manassas (Bull Run)

In the early summer of 1861 the partly trained 90-day militia, the almost untrained volunteers, and one newly organized battalion of Regulars—a total force of 50,000 Federals commanded by Brig. Gen. Irvin McDowell—defended the nation's capital. Thirty miles to the southwest, covering the rail and road hub at Manassas, Virginia, General Beauregard posted some 20,000 Confederates, to be joined by 2,000 more within a few days. To the left, on their defensive line along the Potomac, the Confederates stationed another 11,000 men under Brig. Gen. Joseph E. Johnston in the Shenandoah Valley town of Winchester. Opposing Johnston around Martinsburg, with the mission of keeping the Confederates in place, was Maj. Gen. Robert Patterson with 18,000 Federals. On the extreme right of the Confederate northern Virginia defense line was Col. Joseph B. Magruder's force, which had recently repulsed Maj. Gen. Benjamin F. Butler's Union troops at Big Bethel, Virginia, on 10 June, and forced them back into their sanctuary at Fort Monroe.

Big Bethel, the first large-scale meeting engagement of the Civil War, demonstrated that neither opponent was as yet well trained. The Confederates had started preparations earlier to protect northern Virginia and therefore might have had a slight edge on their opponents. General McDowell, only recently a major of Regulars, had less than three months to weld his three types of units—militia, volunteer, and Regular—into a single fighting force. He attempted to do too much himself, and there were few competent staff officers in the vicinity to help him. McDowell's largest tactical unit was a regiment until just before he marched out of Alexandria. Two to four brigades, plus a battery of Regular artillery—the best arm against raw infantry—formed a division. In all, thirteen brigades were organized into five divisions. McDowell parceled out his forty-nine guns among his brigade commanders, who in turn attached them to their regiments. His total force for the advance was 35,732 men, but of these one division of 5,752 men dropped off to guard roads to the rear.

McDowell's advance against Beauregard, on four parallel routes, was hastened by northern opinion, expressed in editorials and Congressional speeches, demanding immediate action. Scott warned Lincoln against undertaking the "On to Richmond" campaign until McDowell's troops had become disciplined units. But Lincoln, eager to use the 90-day militia before they departed, demanded an advance, being aware that the Confederates were also unseasoned and cherishing the belief that one defeat would force the South to quit. Scott, influenced by false intelligence that Beauregard would move immediately on Washington, acceded. Accordingly, McDowell's battle plan and preparations were expedited. The plan, accepted in late June, called for Butler and Patterson to prevent the Confederates facing them from reinforcing Beauregard, while McDowell advanced against Manassas to outflank the southern position. Scott called it a good plan on paper but knew Johnston was capable of frustrating it if given the chance. McDowell's success against the Confederate center depended upon a rapid 30-mile march, if 35,000 Federals were to keep 22,000 Confederates from being reinforced.

On July 16, 1861, the largest army ever assembled on the North American continent up to that time advanced slowly on both sides of the Warrenton pike toward Bull Run. McDowell's march orders were good, but the effect was ruined by one unwise caution to the brigade commanders: "It will not be pardonable in any commander ... to come upon a battery or breastwork without a knowledge of its position." The caution recalled to McDowell's subordinates the currently sensationalized bugbear of the press of being fooled by "masked batteries," a term originating at Sumter where a certain battery was constructed, masked by a house which was demolished just before the guns opened fire. Accordingly, 35,000 men moved just five miles on the 17th. Next day the Federals occupied Centreville, some four miles east of Stone Bridge, which carried the Warrenton pike over Bull Run. *(Map 3)*

Beauregard's advanced guards made no effort to delay the Federals, but fell back across the battle line, now extending some three miles along the west bank of Bull Run, which meandered from Stone Bridge southeast until it joined the Occoquan stream. The country was fairly rough, cut by streams, and thickly wooded. It presented formidable obstacles to attacking raw troops, but a fair shelter for equally raw troops on the defensive. On the 18th, while McDowell's main body waited at Centreville for the trains to close up, the leading division demonstrated against Beauregard's right around Mitchell's Ford. The Federal infantry retired after a sharp musketry fight, and a 45-minute artillery duel ensued. It was the first exchange of four standard types of artillery ammunition for all muzzle-loading guns, whether rifled or smoothbore. Solid shot, shell, spherical case or shrapnel, and canister from eight Federal guns firing 415 rounds were answered by seven Confederate pieces returning 310 rounds. Steadily withdrawing its guns, the oldest and best drilled unit of the South, the Washington Light Artillery of New Orleans, broke off the fight against well-trained U.S. Regular artillery. Both sides had used rifled artillery, which greatly increased the accuracy and gave a range more than double that of the smoothbores. Yet rifled guns never supplanted the new, easily loaded Napoleons. In the fight, defective Confederate ammunition fired from three new 3-inch iron rifles would not fly point foremost but tumbled and lost range against McDowell's gunners. That the error went undetected for days

16

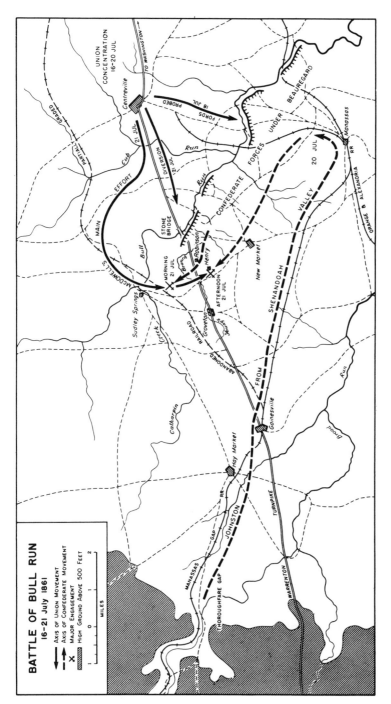

BATTLE OF BULL RUN
16–21 July 1861

Axis of Union Movement
Axis of Confederate Movement
X Major Engagement
High Ground Above 500 Feet

MILES
0   1   2

Map 3

reveals the haste in which Davis had procured his ordnance.

Sure that his green troops could not flank the Confederate right, McDowell tarried two more fateful days before he attacked in force. Engineers reconnoitered for an undefended ford north of Stone Bridge. Finding no vedettes at the ford near Sudley Springs, McDowell decided to envelop the Confederate left on July 21 and destroy the Manassas Gap Railroad to keep Johnston from reinforcing the outnumbered Beauregard. The idea was excellent, but the timing was slow.

While McDowell frittered away four and a half days before he was ready to envelop in force, new tools of warfare swung the advantages of mobility, surprise, and mass at critical points toward Beauregard. On July 17 spies in Washington told of McDowell's departure from Alexandria. By electric telegraph Beauregard in turn alerted Richmond. Davis, also telegraphing, ordered commanders around Richmond, at Aquia Creek, and at Winchester to concentrate their available strength at Manassas. Johnston lost no time in deceiving Patterson by using Col. J. E. B. Stuart's cavalry as a screen and adroitly maneuvering his infantry away from the valley. Johnston selected the best overland routes for his artillery and cavalry marches and arranged for railroad officials to move his four infantry brigades. Brig. Gen. Thomas Jackson's lead brigade, accompanied by Johnston himself, covered fifty-seven miles in twenty-five hours by road and rail, reaching Beauregard on the 20th.

At daylight on the 21st, McDowell unmasked the first phase of his attack plan. Three brigades of Brig. Gen. Daniel Tyler's division appeared before Stone Bridge, and a huge 30-pounder Parrott rifle dragged into place by ten horses commenced a slow fire, directed by six cannoneers of the 2d U.S. Artillery. Five brigades in two divisions directly under McDowell's command meanwhile marched on an eight-mile circuitous route toward the undefended ford at Sudley Springs. McDowell's goal was the Confederate left rear and a chance to cut the railroad. At 9 A.M. a signal flag wigwag from the Henry house announced the point of the enveloping columns at Sudley's crossing, and the intelligence was immediately relayed to Beauregard and Johnston, who were three miles away on the Confederate right.

The first weight of the Federal attack fell against eleven

18

Confederate companies and two guns. For an hour McDowell's regiments, firing one by one and moving forward cautiously in piecemeal fashion, tried to overrun Beauregard's left flank. The timid tactics gave Beauregard time to redeploy ten regiments across a three-mile front to form a second defensive line across the north face of the hill behind the Henry house. At 10:30 A.M., as the summer sun grew hotter, a portentous dust cloud, rising ten miles northwest of Manassas, heralded the arrival of Kirby Smith's brigade, the tail of Johnston's reinforcements from the Shenandoah Valley.

For two hours the roar of the battle swelled in volume. Federal musketry crashes and the thunder from the heavier pieces indicated that McDowell was now committing whole brigades, supported by four batteries of artillery. North of the Warrenton turnpike, the Confederate infantry began to lose its brigade cohesion and fall back in disorder. As Beauregard and Johnston rode to the sound of battle, some 10,000 Federals were punishing 7,000 Confederates in the vicinity of the Henry and Robinson houses. Johnston, though senior in command, turned the battle over to Beauregard and galloped off toward Manassas to direct the arrival of reinforcements. Brig. Gen. Barnard E. Bee's brigade was pushed back from its advanced position toward the flat-crested hill behind the Henry house, where Jackson's newly arrived brigade had formed. In rallying his routed troops, Bee shouted: "Look at Jackson's Brigade; it stands like a stone wall! Rally behind the Virginians!" (Out of these words came a nickname that Jackson would carry to his grave, and after his death in 1863 the Confederate War Department officially designated his unit the Stonewall Brigade.) Screened by a wooded area, three brigades regrouped behind Jackson's lines, and the rally became a great equalizer as McDowell's strength dissipated to 9,000 men, with no immediate infantry reserves in sight.

The cloud of dust moved closer to Manassas Junction, but McDowell ignored it and allowed a lull to settle over his front for almost two hours. At 2 P.M., having deployed two batteries of Regular artillery directly to his front around the Henry house with insufficient infantry protection, McDowell renewed the battle. By midafternoon the dust had blended sweaty uniforms

19

into a common hue, and more and more cases of mistaken identity were confusing both sides in the smoke of the battle. Then, as part of the confusion came a fateful episode. To the right front of McDowell's exposed artillery, a line of advancing blue-clad infantry, the 33d Regiment, Virginia Volunteers suddenly appeared through the smoke. The Federal artillery commander ordered canister, but the chief artillery officer on McDowell's staff overruled the order, claiming that the oncoming blue uniforms belonged to friendly infantry arriving in support. The Virginians advanced to within seventy yards of the Federal guns, leveled their muskets, and let loose. The shock of their volley cut the artillery to shreds, and for the remainder of the day nine Federal guns stood silent, unserved, and helpless between the armies.

About 4 P.M., Beauregard, with two additional fresh brigades, advanced his entire line. Shorn of their artillery, the faltering Federal lines soon lost cohesion and began to pull back along the routes they knew; there was more and more confusion as they retired. East of Bull Run, Federal artillery, using Napoleon smoothbores in this initial pullback from the field, proved to the unsuspecting Confederate cavalry, using classic saber-charging tactics, that a determined line of artillerymen could reduce cavalry to dead and sprawling infantry in minutes.

As in so many battles of the Civil War yet to come, there was no organized pursuit in strength to cut the enemy to ribbons while he fled from the immediate area of the battlefield. At Bull Run the Federal withdrawal turned into a panic-stricken flight about 6:30 P.M., when Cub Run bridge, about a mile west of Centreville, was blocked by overturned wagons. Sunset would fall at 7:15 P.M., and President Davis, just arrived from Richmond, had two daylight hours to arrive at a decision for pursuit. In council with Johnston and Beauregard, Davis instructed the whole Confederate right to advance against the Centreville road, but apparently his orders were never delivered or Beauregard neglected to follow them. Davis thus lost a splendid opportunity for seeing in person whether the unused infantry and artillery on the right of his line could have made a concerted effort to destroy McDowell's fleeing forces. Logistically, Federal booty taken over the next two days by the

20

Confederates would have sustained them for days in an advance against Washington.

Strategically, Bull Run was important to the Confederates only because the center of their Virginia defenses had held. Tactically, the action highlights many of the problems and deficiencies that were typical of the first year of the war. Bull Run was a clash between large, ill-trained bodies of recruits, who were slow in joining battle; masked batteries frightened commanders; plans called for maneuvering the enemy out of position, but attacks were frontal; security principles were disregarded; tactical intelligence was nil; and reconnaissance was poorly executed. Soldiers were overloaded for battle. Neither commander was able to employ his whole force effectively. Of McDowell's 35,000 men, only 18,000 crossed Bull Run and casualties among these, including the missing, numbered about 2,708. Beauregard, with 32,000 men, ordered only 18,000 into action and lost 1,982.

Both commanders rode along the front, often interfering in small unit actions. McDowell led his enveloping column instead of directing all his forces from the rear. Wisely, Johnston left the battlefield and went to the rear to hasten up his Shenandoah Valley reserves. Regiments were committed piecemeal. Infantry failed to protect exposed artillery. Artillery was parceled out under infantry command; only on the retreat was the Union senior artillery officer on the scene allowed to manage his guns. He saved 21 guns of the 49 that McDowell had. Beauregard's orders were oral, vague, and confusing. Some were delivered, others were never followed.

The Second Uprising in 1861

The southern victory near Manassas had an immediate and a long-range effect on the efforts of both the northern and the southern states. First, it compelled northern leaders to face up to the nature and scope of the struggle and to begin the task of putting the Union on a full war footing. Second, it made them more willing to give heed to the advice of professional soldiers charged with the task of directing military operations along a vast continental land front extending from Point Lookout, Maryland, to Fort Craig in central New Mexico. Third, Confederate leaders, after their feeling of invincibility quickly wore off, called for 400,000 volunteers, sought critical military items in Europe, and turned to planning operations that might swing the remaining slaveholding states and territories into the Confederacy. Finally, the most potent immediate influence of Bull Run was upon the European powers, which eyed the Confederacy as a belligerent with much potential for political intervention and as a source of revenue. Unless the Federal Navy could make it unprofitable for private merchant ships to deliver arms to southern ports and depart with agricultural goods, speculative capital would flow increasingly into the contraband trade.

Strategically, in 1861 the U.S. Navy made the most important contribution toward an ultimate Union victory. At considerable expense and in haste to make the blockade effective, the Navy by the end of the year had assembled 200 ships of every description, armed them after a fashion, and placed them on station. With new Congressional acts regarding piracy, revenue, confiscation, and enforcement in hand, commanders of this motley fleet intercepted more and more swift blockade runners steaming out of Nassau, Bermuda, and Havana on their three-day run to Wilmington, North Carolina, Charleston, South Carolina, or Savannah, Georgia. In two round trips a blockade runner, even if lost on its third voyage, still produced a considerable profit to its owner. By the end of 1861 such profit was no longer easy, because the Navy had many new fast ships in service, specially fitted for blockade duty.

After 1861 the naval character of the war changed. There was no Civil War on the high seas except for the exciting exploits of three or four Confederate cruisers which raided commercial shipping. As the war progressed, both opponents perfected the nature and construction of ships and naval ordnance for a war that would be fought in coastal waters or inside defensible harbors. The three main weapons, the rifled naval gun, the armored ram, and the torpedo mine, were developed and used in novel ways. To offset the defensive use of these weapons by the South, the Federal Navy beginning in August 1861 landed more and more Army expeditionary forces and gradually obtained footholds in the vicinity of Mobile, Savannah, Charleston, and Wilmington. By the end of the war, joint Navy-Army expeditions would convert the sea blockade into a military occupation and would seal off all major ports in the South.

The defeat at Bull Run was followed by "a second uprising" in the North, greatly surpassing the effort after Sumter's surrender. President Lincoln and Congress set to with a will to raise and train the large Federal armies that would be required to defeat the South, to select competent Army field commanders, and to reorganize and strengthen the War Department. On July 22, 1861, Lincoln called for a 500,000-man force of 3-year volunteers and during the rest of July quickly disbanded the 90-day militiamen. The more experienced entered the newly authorized volunteer force. Meanwhile, the volunteer quota and the increase of Regulars, mobilized after Sumter, had so far progressed that camps and garrisons, established at strategic points along the 1,950-mile boundary with the border states and territories, were bustling with activity. As July ended, Congress authorized the volunteers to serve for the duration of the war and perfected their regimental organization. Four regiments were grouped into a brigade, and three brigades formed a division. The infantry corps structure would be fixed when the President directed. In effect, the Lincoln administration was building a Federal force, as opposed to one based on joint state-Federal control and support. State governors, given a quota according to a state's population, raised 1,000-man volunteer regiments, bought locally whatever the units needed, shipped them to Federal training centers, and presented all bills to the U.S. Government. Accordingly, Congress floated a national loan of $250 million.

Pending the transformation of their volunteer forces, both opponents suspended major military operations for the remainder of 1861. President Lincoln conferred frequently with General Scott and his military advisers about steps already taken to strengthen Union forces along the continental front. Regular Army units were consolidating their position at Forts Craig and Union to protect the upper Rio Grande valley against any Confederate columns coming from Texas. To protect communication lines to the Pacific and the southwest and to guard Federal supplies at Fort Leavenworth, Kansas, and St. Louis, Missouri, Union troops were deployed in eastern Kansas and across central Missouri. In August Union troops fought a drawn battle at Wilson's Creek, and Missouri became a state divided against itself. The loss of Kentucky, in Lincoln's judgment, would be "nearly the same as to lose the whole game"; so he carefully respected Kentucky's decision of May to remain neutral. After Bull Run, Illinois, Indiana, and Ohio volunteers were assembled north of the Ohio at exposed river towns to keep watch on the situation in Kentucky. In western Virginia forty counties elected to secede from Virginia and asked for Federal troops to assist them in repelling any punitive expeditions emerging from the Shenandoah Valley. Between May and early July 1861, Ohio volunteers, under the command of Maj. Gen. George B. McClellan, occupied the Grafton area of western Virginia, hoping to protect the railroad that linked the Ohio Valley with Baltimore. In a series of clashes at Philippi, Beverly, and along the Cheat River, McClellan's forces checked the invading Confederates, paving the way for West Virginia's entrance into the Union.

Although the border strife intensified in the west, Scott attended to the more important front facing Virginia. The nation's capital was imperiled, the Potomac was directly under Confederate guns, and Maryland and Delaware were being used as recruiting areas for the southern cause. On July 22, Lincoln following Scott's advice, had summoned McClellan, who was thirty-five years old at the time, to Washington, and assigned him command, under Scott, of all the troops in the Washington area. McClellan's reputation was unrivaled, and the public had acclaimed him for his victories in western Virginia. On August 21 McClellan named his force the Army of the Potomac, and commenced molding it into a formidable machine.

McClellan organized the Army of the Potomac into eleven 10,000-man divisions, each with three brigades of infantry, a cavalry regiment, and four six-gun batteries. In general this structure was adopted by the other Union armies, and the Confederates deviated from the model only in their cavalry organization. In the Army of Northern Virginia, for example,

24

General Lee treated his cavalry as a tactical arm, grouped first as a division, and later as a cavalry corps. Union cavalry consisted of little more than mounted infantry, carrying out a multitude of duties for the division commander, such as serving as pickets, wagon train escorts, and couriers. McClellan planned, once Lincoln activated corps, to withdraw one-half of the artillery pieces from each infantry division and center them at corps level as a reserve to be deployed under army command. He insisted that the .58-caliber single-shot, muzzle-loading Springfield rifle be the standard weapon of the infantry, and most of the Army of the Potomac possessed it when corps were organized on March 8, 1862.

McClellan completely transformed the military atmosphere around Washington before the end of 1861. Although he was an able administrator, his critics doubted his abilities as a top field commander. From the day he activated the Army of the Potomac, McClellan was politically active in trying to oust Scott. Finally, on November 1, the aged and harassed General in Chief, taking advantage of a new law, retired from the Army. That same day, acting on assurances that McClellan could handle two tasks concurrently, Lincoln made McClellan the General in Chief and retained him in command of the Army of the Potomac. By the 9th, basing his action on Scott's earlier groundwork, McClellan carved out five new departments in the west, all commanded by Regular Army officers. In addition, he continued the work of the new Department of New England, where General Butler was already forming volunteer regiments for scheduled seaborne operations off the Carolina capes and in the Gulf of New Mexico.

For the Union cause in Kentucky, the new General in Chief's move came none too soon. As early as September 4, a Confederate force from Tennessee had violated Kentucky's neutrality by occupying the Mississippi River town and railroad terminal of Columbus. The next day Illinois troops under Brig. Gen. Ulysses S. Grant seized Paducah and Smithland, strategic river towns in Kentucky at the confluence of the Tennessee and Cumberland Rivers with the Ohio. After Kentucky declared for the Union on September 20, both sides rapidly concentrated forces in western Kentucky. Maj. Gen. Albert S. Johnston, recently appointed to command Confederate forces in the west, fortified Bowling Green, Kentucky, and extended his defensive line to Columbus. Union troops immediately occupied Louisville and planned advances down the railroad to Nashville and eastward into the Appalachians. By November 15, the commanders of the Department of the Ohio and the Department of the Missouri, dividing their operational boundaries in Kentucky along the Cumberland River, were exchanging strategic plans with McClellan in anticipation of a grand offensive in the spring of 1862.

The outpouring of troops and their preparations for battle disrupted the leisurely pace of the War Department. In their haste to supply, equip, and deploy the second quota of volunteers, a score or more of states competed not only against one another but against the Federal government as well. Profiteers demanded exorbitant prices for scarce items, which frequently turned out to be worthless. Unbridled graft and extravagance were reflected in the bills which the states presented to the War Department for payment. After Bull Run a concerted, widespread movement emerged for the dismissal of Secretary of War Simon Cameron, who had failed to manage his office efficiently. Cameron selected Edwin M. Stanton, former Attorney General in President Buchanan's cabinet, as his special counsel to handle all legal arguments justifying the War Department's purchasing policies. Knowing that the cabinet post had considerable potential, Stanton worked hard to restore the War Department's prestige. Behind the scenes Stanton aided his fellow Democrat, McClellan, in outfitting the Army of the Potomac. As the summer faded Stanton, having once scoffed at Lincoln early in the war, ingratiated himself with the President and his key cabinet members by urging his pro-Union views. In January 1862 Lincoln replaced Cameron with Stanton, who immediately set out to make his cabinet position the most powerful in Lincoln's administration.

Self-confident, arrogant, abrupt, and contemptuous of incompetent military leaders, Stanton was also fiercely energetic, incorruptible, and efficient. Respecting few men and fearing none, he did his best to eliminate favoritism and see to it that war contracts were honestly negotiated and faithfully filled. Few men liked Stanton, but almost all high officials respected him. Stanton insisted that the Army receive whatever it needed, and the best available, and no campaign by any Union army would ever fail for want of supplies.

From the day that Stanton took office, the structure of the War Department was centralized to handle the growing volume of business. Each bureau chief reported directly to Stanton, but the responsibility became so heavy that he delegated procurement and distribution matters to three assistant secretaries. Because the Quartermaster General's Department transported men and matériel, operated the depot system, constructed camps, and handled the largest number of contracts, it soon became the most important agency of the general staff. Hardworking, efficient, and loyal, Montgomery C. Meigs as Quartermaster General was an organizing genius, and was one of the few career officers to whom Stanton would listen. To complete his department, Stanton added three major bureaus during the war: the Judge Advocate General's Office in 1862; the Signal Department in 1863; and the Provost Marshal General's Bureau, established in 1863 to administer the draft (enrollment) act. In the same year the Corps of Topographical Engineers was merged with the Corps of Engineers.

Stanton faced mobilization problems and home front crises of unprecedented magnitude. Loyal states were bringing half a million men under arms. Grain, wool, leather, lumber, metals, and fuel were being turned into food, clothing, vehicles, and guns, and thousands of draft animals were being purchased and shipped from every part of the North. A well-managed Federal authority was needed to assume the states' obligations, to train volunteer units in the use of their tools of war, and then to deploy them along a vast continental front. By exploiting the railroad, steamship, and telegraph, the War Department provided field commanders a novel type of mobility in their operations. Stanton's major task was to control all aspects of this outpouring of the nation's resources. If war contracts were tainted, the Union soldiers might despair. Moral as well as financial bankruptcy could easily wreck Union hopes of victory. In addition, Stanton had the job of suppressing subversion, of timing the delicate matter of putting Negroes in the Army, and of co-operating with a radical-dominated Congress, a strong-willed cabinet, and a conservative-minded Army. With a lawyer's training, Stanton, like Lincoln, knew little about military affairs, and there was little time for him to learn. Anticipating that President Lincoln would soon call for War Department plans for the spring 1862 offensives, Stanton researched every document he could find on Army administration, consulted his bureau chiefs about readiness, and prepared himself to work with the General in Chief on strategic matters.

When he took office, Stanton found that the War Department had a rival in the form of the Joint Congressional Committee on the Conduct of the War. It had its origins in an investigation of a badly executed reconnaissance at Ball's Bluff on the Potomac, October 21, 1861, in which a volunteer officer and popular former senator, Col. Edward D. Baker, was killed. By subsequently searching out graft and inefficiency, the committee did valuable service, but it also vexed the President, Stanton, and most of the generals during the war. Composed of extreme antislavery men without military knowledge and experience, the committee probed the battles, tried to force all its views regarding statecraft and strategy on the President, and put forward its own candidates for high command. Suspicious of proslavery men and men of moderate views, it considered that the only generals fit for office were those who had been abolitionists before 1861.

As the year ended both North and South were earnestly preparing for a hard war. Both opponents were raising and training huge armies totaling nearly a million men. Fort Sumter and bloody Bull Run were over and each side was gathering its resources for the even bloodier struggles to come.

CHAPTER 2

1862

In 1862 the armed forces of the United States undertook the first massive campaigns to defeat the southern Confederacy. Better organization, training, and leadership would be displayed on both sides as the combat became more intense. Young American citizen soldiers would find that war was not a romantic adventure and their leaders would learn that every victory had its price.

As the winter of 1861–62 wore on, McClellan exaggerated his difficulties and the enemy's strength, and discounted the Confederacy's problems. He drilled and trained the Army of the Potomac while western forces under his general command accomplished little. Lincoln and the Union waited impatiently for a conclusive engagement. But neither the Union nor the Confederate Army showed much inclination to move, each being intent on perfecting itself before striking a heavy blow.

The President was particularly eager to support Unionist sentiment in east Tennessee by moving forces in that direction. Above all he wanted a concerted movement to crush the rebellion quickly. In an effort to push matters Lincoln issued General War Order No. 1 on January 27, 1862. This order, besides superfluously telling the armies to obey existing orders, directed that a general movement of land and sea forces against the Confederacy be launched on February 22, 1862. Lincoln's issuance of an order for an offensive several weeks in advance, without considering what the weather and the roads might be like, has been scoffed at frequently. But apparently he issued it only to get McClellan to agree to move. Even before Lincoln sent the directive his intentions were overtaken by events in the western theater.

The Twin Rivers Campaign

Students of the Civil War often concentrate their study upon the cockpit of the war in the east—Virginia. The rival capitals lay only a hundred miles apart and the country between them was fought over for four years. But it was the Union armies west of the Appalachians that struck the death knell of the Confederacy.

These Union forces in late 1861 were organized into two separate commands. Brig. Gen. Don Carlos Buell commanded some 45,000 men from a headquarters at Louisville, Kentucky, while Maj. Gen. Henry W. Halleck with headquarters at St. Louis, Missouri, had 91,000 under his command. These troops were generally raw, undisciplined western volunteers. Logistical matters and training facilities were undeveloped and as Halleck once wrote in disgust to his superior in Washington, "affairs here are in complete chaos."

Affairs were no better among Confederate authorities farther south. Facing Buell and Halleck were 43,000 scattered and ill-equipped Confederate troops under General Albert Sidney Johnston. Charged with defending a line which stretched for more than 500 miles from western Virginia to the border of Kansas, Johnston's forces mostly lay east of the Mississippi River. They occupied a system of forts and camps from Cumberland Gap in western Virginia through Bowling Green, Kentucky, to Columbus, Kentucky, on the Mississippi. Rivers and railroads provided Johnston with most of his interior lines of communications since most of the roads were virtually impassable in winter. To protect a lateral railroad where it crossed two rivers in Tennessee and yet respect Kentucky's neutrality, the Confederates had built Fort Henry on the Tennessee River and Fort Donelson on the Cumberland River just south of the boundary between the two states. On the other hand, hampering the Confederate build-up were southern governors whose states' rights doctrine led them to believe that defense of their respective states had higher priority than pushing forward the needed men and munitions to a Confederate commander, Johnston, at the front.

At the beginning of 1862, Halleck and Buell were supposed to

30

GENERAL U. S. GRANT

be co-operating with each other but had yet to do so effectively. On his own, Buell moved in mid-January to give token response to Lincoln's desire to help the Unionists in east Tennessee. One of his subordinates succeeded in breaching the Confederate defense line in eastern Kentucky in a local action near Mill Springs, but Buell failed to exploit the victory.

In Halleck's department, Brig. Gen. Ulysses S. Grant, at the time an inconspicuous district commander at Cairo, Illinois, had meanwhile proposed a river expedition up the Tennessee to take Fort Henry. After some hesitancy and in spite of the absence of assurance of support from Buell, Halleck approved a plan for a joint Army-Navy expedition. On January 30, 1862, he directed 15,000 men under Grant, supported by armored gunboats and river craft of the U.S. Navy under Flag Officer Andrew H. Foote, to "take and hold Fort Henry." The actions of subordinate commanders were at last prodding the Union war machine to move.

Capture of Forts Henry and Donelson

Grant landed his troops below Fort Henry and together with Foote's naval force moved against the Confederate position on February 6. At the Federals' approach the Confederate commander sent most of his men to Fort Donelson. Muddy roads delayed the Union Army's advance, but Foote's seven gunboats plunged ahead and in a short fire fight induced the defenders of Fort Henry to surrender. Indeed, the Confederates had lowered their colors before Grant's infantry could reach the action. The Tennessee River now lay open to Foote's gunboats all the way to northern Alabama.

General Grant was no rhetorician. Sparing with words, he never bombarded his troops with Napoleonic manifestos as McClellan did. After the capture of Fort Henry he simply telegraphed the somewhat surprised Halleck: "I shall take and destroy Fort Donelson on the 8th and return to Fort Henry." But inclement weather delayed the Federal movement until February 12. Then river craft carried some of the troops by water around to Fort Donelson. The rest of the troops moved overland under sunny skies and unseasonably mild temperatures. The springlike weather caused the youthful soldiers to litter the roadside with overcoats, blankets, and tents.

But winter once more descended upon Grant's forces (soon to swell to nearly 27,000 men) as they invested Fort Donelson. Johnston, sure that the fall of this fort would jeopardize his entrenched camp at Bowling Green, hurried three generals and 12,000 reinforcements to Fort Donelson and then retired toward Nashville with 14,000 men. Even without reinforcements, Fort Donelson was a strong position. The main earthwork stood 100 feet above the river and with its outlying system of rifle pits embraced an area of 100 acres. The whole Confederate position occupied less than a square mile. Grant and Foote first attempted to reduce it by naval bombardment, which had succeeded at Fort Henry. But this time the Confederate defenders handled the gunboats so roughly that they withdrew. Grant then prepared for a long siege, although the bitter cold weather and lack of assault training among his troops caused him to have some reservations.

The Confederates, sensing they were caught in a trap, essayed a sortie on February 15, and swept one of Grant's divisions off the field. But divided Confederate command, not lack of determination or valor on the part of the fighting men, led to ultimate defeat of the attack. The three Confederate commanders could not agree upon the next move, and at a critical moment, Grant ordered counterattacks all along the line. By the end of the day Union troops had captured a portion of the Confederate outer works. Now surrounded by Union forces that outnumbered them almost two to one, the Confederate leaders decided they were in a hopeless situation. In a scene resembling *opéra bouffe*, Brig. Gen. John B. Floyd, who had been Buchanan's Secretary of War and feared execution as a traitor, passed the command to Brig. Gen. Gideon Pillow. Pillow passed the command immediately to Brig. Gen. Simon B. Buckner, who asked Grant, an old friend, for terms. Soon afterward Grant sent his famous message: "No terms except unconditional and immediate surrender can be accepted. I propose to move immediately upon your works."

Some Confederates escaped with Floyd and Pillow, and Col. Nathan Bedford Forrest led his cavalry through frozen backwaters to safety. But the bulk of the garrison "from 12,000 to 15,000 prisoners . . . also 20,000 stand of arms, 48 pieces of artillery, 17 heavy guns, from 2,000 to 4,000 horses, and large quantities of commissary stores" fell into Federal hands.

Poor leadership, violation of the principle of unity of command, and too strict adherence to position defense had cost the South the key to the gateway of the Confederacy in the west. The loss of the two forts dealt the Confederacy a blow from which it never fully recovered. Johnston had to abandon Kentucky and most of middle and west Tennessee. The vital industrial and transportation center of Nashville soon fell to Buell's advancing army. Foreign governments took special notice of the defeats. For the North the victories were its first good news of the war. They set the strategic pattern for further advance into the Confederacy. In Grant the people had a new hero and he was quickly dubbed "Unconditional Surrender" Grant.

Confederate Counterattack at Shiloh

As department commander, Halleck naturally received much credit for these victories. President Lincoln decided to unify command of all the western armies, and on March 11 Halleck received the command. Halleck, nicknamed "Old Brains," was well known as a master of the theory and literature of war. Lincoln's decision gave him jurisdiction over four armies— Buell's Army of the Ohio, Grant's Army of the Tennessee, Maj. Gen. Samuel Curtis' Army of the Southwest in Missouri and Arkansas, and Maj. Gen. John Pope's Army of the Mississippi. While Pope, in co-operation with Foote's naval forces, successfully attacked New Madrid and Island No. 10 on the Mississippi River, Halleck decided to concentrate Grant's and Buell's armies and move against Johnston at Corinth in northern Mississippi. Grant and Buell were to meet at Shiloh (Pittsburg Landing) near Savannah on the Tennessee River. Well aware of the Federal movements, Johnston decided to attack Grant before Buell could join him. *(Map 4)* The Confederate army, 40,000 strong, marched out of Corinth on the afternoon of April 3. Muddy roads and faulty staff co-ordination made a shambles of Confederate march discipline. Mixed up commands, artillery and wagons bogged down in the mud, and green troops who insisted upon shooting their rifles at every passing rabbit threatened to abort the whole expedition. Not until late in the afternoon of April 5 did Johnston's army complete the 22-mile march to its attack point. Then the Confederate leader postponed his attack until the next morning and the delay proved costly.

Grant's forces were encamped in a rather loose battle line and apparently anticipated no attack. The position at Shiloh itself was not good, for the army was pocketed by the river at its back

34

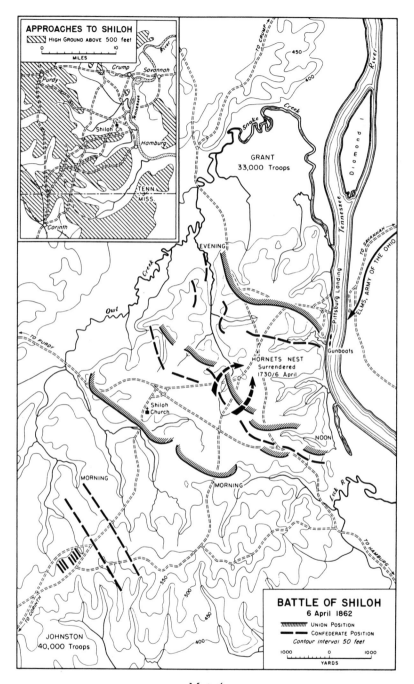

APPROACHES TO SHILOH

▨ HIGH GROUND ABOVE 500 feet

0   MILES   10

Crump
Savannah
Purdy
Tennessee River
Shiloh Ch.
Hamburg
TENN.
MISS.
Corinth

GRANT
33,000 Troops

Snake Creek

Diamond I.

Tennessee River

TO CRUMP

450

600

TO SAVANNAH

Pittsburg Landing

ELMS, ARMY OF THE OHIO

EVENING

Owl Creek

TO PURDY

HORNETS NEST
Surrendered
1730/6 April

Gunboats

Shiloh
Church

NOON

MORNING

MORNING

Lick R.

TO HAMBURG

550

500

450

400

TO CORINTH

JOHNSTON
40,000 Troops

BATTLE OF SHILOH
6 April 1862

▨▨▨▨ UNION POSITION
▬ ▬ ▬ CONFEDERATE POSITION
Contour interval 50 feet

1000   0   1000
YARDS

Map 4

and a creek on each flank. Because the army was on an offensive mission, it had not entrenched. Grant has often been criticized for this omission, but entrenchment was not common at that stage of the war. The fact that the principle of security was disregarded is inescapable. Very little patrolling had been carried out, and the Federals were unaware that a Confederate army of 40,000 men was spending the night of April 5 just two miles away. The victories at Forts Henry and Donelson had apparently produced overconfidence in Grant's army, which like Johnston's, was only partly trained. Even Grant reflected this feeling, for he had established his headquarters at Savannah, nine miles downstream.

Johnston's men burst out of the woods early on April 6, so early that Union soldiers turned out into their company streets from their tents to fight. Some fled to the safety of the landing, but most of the regiments fought stubbornly and yielded ground slowly. One particular knot of Federals rallied along an old sunken road, named the Hornet's Nest by Confederates because of the stinging shot and shell they had to face there. Although this obstacle disrupted Johnston's timetable of attack, by afternoon the Confederates had attained local success elsewhere all along the line. At the same time the melee of battle badly disorganized the attackers. Johnston's attack formation had been awkward from the beginning. He had formed his three corps into one column with each corps deployed with divisions in line so that each corps stretched across the whole battlefront, one behind the other. Such a formation could be effectively controlled neither by army nor corps commanders.

Then, almost at the moment of victory, Johnston himself was mortally wounded while leading a local assault. General Beauregard, Johnston's successor, suspended the attack for the day and attempted to straighten out and reorganize his command. As the day ended, Grant's sixth division, which had lost its way while marching to the battlefield, reached Shiloh along with advance elements of Buell's army.

Next morning Grant counterattacked to regain the lost ground and the Confederates withdrew to Corinth. There was no pursuit. Shiloh was the bloodiest battle fought in North America up to that time. Of 63,000 Federals, 13,000 were casualties. The Confederates lost 11,000. Fortunate indeed for the Federals had been Lincoln's decision to unify the command under Halleck, for this act had guaranteed Buell's presence and prevented Johnston from defeating the Union armies separately. Grant came in for much denunciation for being surprised, but President Lincoln loyally sustained him. "I can't spare this man; he fights."

Halleck was a master of military maxims, but he had failed to concentrate all his forces immediately for a final defeat of Beauregard. As it was, Pope and Foote took Island No. 10 in April, opening the Mississippi as far as Memphis. Halleck, taking personal command of Grant's and Buell's forces, then ponderously advanced toward Corinth. Remembering Shiloh, he proceeded cautiously, and it was May 30 before he reached his objective. Beauregard had already evacuated the town. Meanwhile Capt. David G. Farragut with a naval force and Maj. Gen. Benjamin F. Butler's land units cracked the gulf coast fortifications of the Mississippi and captured New Orleans. By mid-1862, only strongholds at Vicksburg and Port Hudson on the Mississippi blocked complete Federal control of that vital river.

Perryville to Stones River

Despite these early setbacks the Confederate armies in the west were still full of fight. As Federal forces advanced deeper into the Confederacy it became increasingly difficult for them to protect the long lines of river, rail, and road supply and communications. Guerrilla and cavalry operations by colorful Confederate "wizards of the saddle" like John Hunt Morgan, Joseph Wheeler, and Nathan Bedford Forrest followed Forrest's adage of "Get 'em skeered, and then keep the skeer on 'em." Such tactics completely disrupted the timetable of Federal offensives.

By summer and fall rejuvenated Confederate forces under General Braxton Bragg, Lt. Gen. Edmund Kirby Smith, and Maj. Gen. Earl Van Dorn were ready to seize the initiative. Never again was the South so close to victory, nor did it ever again hold the initiative in every theater of the war.

Overall Confederate strategy called for a three-pronged

advance from the Mississippi River all the way to Virginia. Twin columns under Bragg and Smith were to bear the brunt of the western offensive by advancing from Chattanooga into east Tennessee, then northward into Kentucky. They were to be supported by Van Dorn, who would move north from Mississippi with the intention of driving Grant's forces out of west Tennessee. The western columns of the Confederacy were then to unite somewhere in Kentucky.

At the same time, these movements were to be co-ordinated with the planned invasion of Maryland, east of the Appalachians, by General Robert E. Lee's Army of Northern Virginia. Much depended upon speed, good co-ordination of effort and communications, and attempts to woo Kentucky and Maryland into the arms of the Confederacy. Victory could stimulate peace advocates and the Copperheads in the North to bring peace. Furthermore there was always the possibility that a successful invasion might induce Great Britain and France to recognize the Confederacy and to intervene forcibly to break the blockade. This last hope was a feeble one. Emperor Napoleon III was primarily interested in advancing his Mexican schemes; he considered both recognition and intervention but would not move without British support. Britain, which pursued the policy of recognizing *de facto* governments, would undoubtedly have recognized the Confederacy eventually had it won the war. But the British Government only briefly flirted with the idea of recognition and throughout the war adhered to a policy of neutrality and respect for the Union blockade.

At first things went well for the Confederates in the west. Bragg caught Buell off guard and without fighting a battle forced Federal evacuation of northern Alabama and central Tennessee. But when Bragg entered Kentucky he became engaged in "government making" in an effort to set up a state regime which would bind Kentucky to the Confederacy. Also, the Confederate invasion was not achieving the expected results since few Kentuckians joined Bragg's forces and an attempt at conscription in east Tennessee failed completely.

Buell finally caught up with Bragg's advance at Perryville, Kentucky, on October 7. Finding the Confederates in some strength, Buell began concentrating his own scattered units. The next morning fighting began around Perryville over possession of drinking water. Brig. Gen. Philip H. Sheridan's division forced the Confederates away from one creek and dug in. The battle as a whole turned out to be a rather confused affair as Buell sought to concentrate units arriving from several different directions upon the battlefield itself. Early in the afternoon, Maj. Gen. Alexander M. McCook's Union corps arrived and began forming a line of battle. At that moment Maj. Gen. Leonidas Polk's Confederate corps attacked and drove McCook back about a mile, but Sheridan's troops held their ground. Finally a Union counterattack pushed the Confederates out of the town of Perryville. Buell himself remained at headquarters, only two and a half miles from the field, completely unaware of the extent of the engagement until it was nearly over. The rolling terrain had caused an "acoustic shadow" whereby the sounds of the conflict were completely inaudible to the Federal commander. While the battle ended in a tactical stalemate, Bragg suffered such severe casualties that he was forced to retreat. Coupled with Van Dorn's failure to bypass Federal defenses at Corinth, Mississippi, and carry out his part of the strategic plan, this setback forced the Confederates to abandon any idea of bringing Kentucky into the Confederacy.

By Christmas Bragg was back in middle Tennessee, battered but still anxious to recoup his losses by recapturing Nashville. Buell had been dilatory in pursuing Bragg after Perryville and had been replaced in command of the Army of the Ohio (now restyled the Army of the Cumberland) by Maj. Gen. William S. Rosecrans. In spite of urgent and even threatening letters from the War Department, the new commander would not move against Bragg until he had collected abundant supplies at Nashville. Then he would be independent of the railroad line from Nashville to Louisville, a line of communications continually cut by Confederate cavalry.

On December 26 Rosecrans finally marched south from Nashville. Poorly screened by Union cavalry, his three columns in turn knew little about Confederate concentrations near Murfreesboro, thirty miles southeast of the Tennessee capital. Here Bragg had taken a strong position astride Stones River on the direct route to Chattanooga and proposed to fight it out.

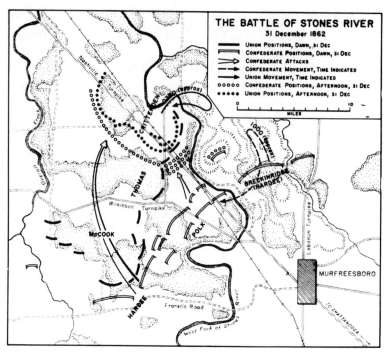

THE BATTLE OF STONES RIVER
31 December 1862

UNION POSITIONS, DAWN, 31 DEC
CONFEDERATE POSITIONS, DAWN, 31 DEC
CONFEDERATE ATTACKS
CONFEDERATE MOVEMENT, TIME INDICATED
UNION MOVEMENT, TIME INDICATED
CONFEDERATE POSITIONS, AFTERNOON, 31 DEC
UNION POSITIONS, AFTERNOON, 31 DEC

0   MILES   10

Map 5

Rosecrans moved into line opposite Bragg on the evening of December 30. Both army commanders proceeded to develop identical battle plans—each designed to envelop the opponent's right flank. Bragg's objective was to drive Rosecrans off his communications line with Nashville and pin him against the river. Rosecrans' plan had the same objective in reverse, that of pinning the Confederates against the stream. Victory would probably belong to the commander who struck first and hard.

Insufficient Federal security and Rosecrans' failure to insure that the pivotal units in his attack plan were also properly posted to thwart Confederate counterattacks resulted in Confederate seizure of the initiative as the battle of Stones River opened on December 31. *(Map 5)* At dawn, Maj. Gen. William J. Hardee's corps with large cavalry support began the drive on the Federal right. Undeceived by their opponent's device of extra campfires to feign a longer battle line, Confederate attacking columns simply pushed farther around the Union flank and promptly rolled the defenders back. Applying the

40

principles of mass and surprise to achieve rapid success, Bragg's battle plan forced Rosecrans to modify his own. The Union leader pulled back his left flank division, which had jumped off to attack Maj. Gen. John C. Breckinridge's Confederate units north of Stones River. While Sheridan's division, as at Perryville, provided stubborn resistance to General Polk's corps in the center, Hardee's units continued their drive, which by noon saw the Union battle line bent back against the Nashville pike. Meanwhile the Confederate cavalry had wrought havoc among Rosecrans' rear area elements. As was typical of many Civil War battles the attacking columns of Polk and Hardee became badly intermingled. Their men began to tire, and by afternoon repeated Confederate assaults against the constricted Union line along the Nashville pike had bogged down.

That night Rosecrans held a council of war. Some of the subordinate commanders wanted to retreat. Rosecrans and two of his corps commanders, Maj. Gen. Thomas L. Crittenden and Maj. Gen. George H. Thomas, vetoed the scheme. Brigades were then returned to their proper divisions, stragglers rounded up, and various other adjustments made in the Federal position. New Year's Day, 1863, dawned quiet and little action occurred that day.

The sunrise of January 2 revealed Rosecrans still in position. Bragg directed Breckinridge to attack the Union left wing, once more thrown across Stones River on the north. But massed Union artillery shattered the assaults and counterattacking Federals drove Breckinridge's men back to their line of departure. The armies remained stationary on January 3 but Bragg finally withdrew from the battlefield that evening, permitting victory to slip from his grasp. Tactically a draw, Stones River so badly mangled the Army of the Cumberland that it would be immobilized for six months. Yet, more than most other battles of the war, Stones River was a conflict between the wills of the opposing army leaders. Rosecrans, supported by Thomas and others, would not admit himself beaten and in the end won a victory of sorts.

The great Confederate counteroffensives of 1862 had failed in the west, yet Chattanooga, the key to east Tennessee and Georgia, remained in southern hands. Farther west Federal forces had penetrated only slightly into northern Mississippi. The war was simply on dead center in the west at the end of the year.

The Army of the Potomac Moves South

As the year 1862 began in the eastern theater, plans prepared in Washington were aimed at the capture of Richmond rather than destruction of the army commanded by Joseph E. Johnston, now a full general. Precise methods for reaching the Confederate capital differed. President Lincoln favored an overland advance which would always keep an army between the Confederates and Washington. McClellan agreed at first, then changed his views in favor of a waterborne move by the Army of the Potomac to Urbana on the Rappahannock. From there he could drive to Richmond before Johnston could retire from the Manassas area to intercept him. The Washington fortifications, an elaborate system of earthen forts and battery emplacements then in advanced stages of construction, would adequately protect the capital while the field army was away. Johnston, however, rendered this plan obsolete; he withdrew from Manassas to Fredericksburg, halfway between the two capitals and astride McClellan's prospective route of advance. Early in March McClellan moved his army out to the deserted Confederate camps around Manassas to give his troops some field experience. While he was in the field President Lincoln relieved him as General in Chief, doubtless on the ground that he could not command one army in the field and at the same time supervise the operations of all the armies of the United States. Lincoln did not appoint a successor. For a time he and Stanton took over personal direction of the Army, with the advice of a newly constituted Army board consisting of the elderly Maj. Gen. Ethan A. Hitchcock and the chiefs of the War Department bureaus.

When events overtook the Urbana scheme, McClellan began to advocate a seaborne move to Fort Monroe, Virginia (at the tip of the peninsula formed by the York and James Rivers), to be followed by an overland advance up the peninsula. If the troops moved fast, he maintained, they could cover the seventy-five miles to Richmond before Johnston could concentrate his forces to stop them. This plan had promise, for it utilized Federal control of the seas and a useful base of operations at Fort Monroe and there were fewer rivers to cross than by the overland route. Successful neutralization of the *Merrimac* by the *Monitor* on March 9 had eliminated any naval threat to supply and communications lines, but the absence of good roads and the difficult terrain of the peninsula offered drawbacks to the plan. Lincoln approved it, providing McClellan would leave behind the number of men that his corps commanders considered adequate to insure the safety of Washington. McClellan gave the President his assurances, but failed to take Lincoln into his confidence by pointing out that he considered the Federal troops in the Shenandoah Valley to be covering Washington. In listing the forces he had left behind, he counted some men twice and included several units in Pennsylvania not under his command.

Embarkation began in mid-March, and by April 4 advance elements had moved out of Fort Monroe against Yorktown. The day before, however, the commander of the Washington defenses reported that he had insufficient forces to protect the city. In addition, Stonewall Jackson had become active in the Shenandoah Valley. Lincoln thereupon told Stanton to detain one of the two corps which were awaiting embarkation at Alexandria. Stanton held back McDowell's corps, numbering 30,000 men, seriously affecting McClellan's plans.

Jackson's Valley Campaign

While a small Confederate garrison at Yorktown made ready to delay McClellan, Johnston hurried his army to the peninsula. In Richmond Confederate authorities had determined on a spectacularly bold diversion. Robert E. Lee, who had rapidly moved to the rank of general, had assumed the position of military adviser to Jefferson Davis on March 13. Charged with the conduct of operations of the Confederate armies under Davis' direction, Lee saw that any threat to Washington would cause progressive weakening of McClellan's advance against Richmond. He therefore ordered Jackson to begin a rapid campaign in the Shenandoah Valley close to the northern capital. The equivalent of three Federal divisions was sent to the valley to destroy Jackson. Lincoln and Stanton, using the telegraph and what military knowledge they had acquired, devised plans to bottle Jackson up and destroy him. But Federal forces in the valley were not under a locally unified command. They moved too slowly; one force did not obey orders strictly; and directives from Washington often neglected to take time, distance, or logistics into account. Also, in Stonewall Jackson, the Union troops were contending against one of the most outstanding field commanders America has ever produced. Jackson's philosophy of war was:

> Always mystify, mislead, and surprise the enemy, if possible; and when you strike and overcome him, never give up the pursuit as long as your men have strength to follow; for an army routed, if hotly pursued, becomes panic-stricken and can then be destroyed by half their number.

By mobility and maneuver, achieved by rapid marches, surprise, deception, and hard fighting, Jackson neutralized and defeated in detail Federal forces three times larger than his own. In a classic campaign between March 23 and June 9, 1862, he fought six battles: Kernstown, McDowell, Front Royal, Winchester, Cross Keys, and Port Republic. All but Kernstown were victories. His presence alone in the Shenandoah immobilized McDowell's corps by keeping these reinforcements from joining McClellan before Richmond.

The Peninsular Campaign: Fair Oaks

When McClellan reached the peninsula in early April he found a force of ten to fifteen thousand Confederates under Maj. Gen. John B. Magruder barring his path to Richmond. Magruder, a student of drama and master of deception, so dazzled him that McClellan, instead of brushing the Confeder-

44

ates aside, spent a month in a siege of Yorktown. But Johnston, who wanted to fight the decisive action closer to Richmond, decided to withdraw slowly up the peninsula. At Williamsburg, on May 5, McClellan's advance elements made contact with the Confederate rear guard under Maj. Gen. James Longstreet, who successfully delayed the Federal advance. McClellan then pursued in leisurely fashion. By May 25, two corps of the Army of the Potomac had turned southwest toward Richmond and crossed the sluggish Chickahominy River. The remaining three corps were on the north side of the stream with the expectation of making contact with McDowell, who would come down from Fredericksburg. Men of the two corps south of the river could see the spires of the Confederate capital, but Johnston's army was in front of them. *(Map 6)*

Drenching rains on May 30 raised the Chickahominy to flood stage and seriously divided McClellan's army. Johnston decided to grasp this chance to defeat the Federals in detail. He struck on May 31 near Fair Oaks. His plans called for his whole force to concentrate against the isolated corps south of the river, but his staff and subordinate commanders were not up to the task of executing them. Assaulting columns became confused, and attacks were delivered piecemeal. The Federals, after some initial reverses, held their ground and bloodily repulsed the Confederates.

When Johnston suffered a severe wound at Fair Oaks, President Davis replaced him with General Lee. Lee for his part had no intention of defending Richmond passively. The city's fortifications would enable him to protect Richmond with a relatively small force while he used the main body of his army offensively in an attempt to cut off and destroy the Army of the Potomac. He ordered Jackson back from the Shenandoah Valley with all possible speed.

The Seven Days' Battles

McClellan had planned to utilize his superior artillery to break through the Richmond defenses, but Lee struck the Federal Army before it could resume the advance. Lee's

45

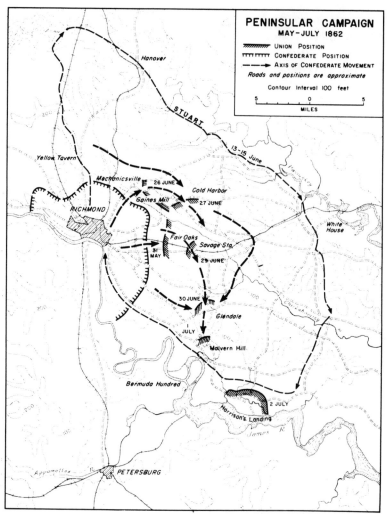

Map 6

dispositions for the Battle of Mechanicsville on June 26 present
a good illustration of the principles of mass and economy of
force. On the north side of the Chickahominy, he concentrated
65,000 men to oppose Brig. Gen. Fitz-John Porter's V Corps of
30,000. Only 25,000 were left before Richmond to contain the
remainder of the Union Army. When Lee attacked, the timing
and co-ordination were off; Jackson of all people was slow and
the V Corps defended stoutly during the day. McClellan

46

thereupon withdrew the V Corps southeast to a stronger position at Gaines' Mill. Porter's men constructed light barricades and made ready. Lee massed 57,000 men and assaulted 34,000 Federals on June 27. The fighting was severe but numbers told, and the Federal line broke. Darkness fell before Lee could exploit his advantage, and McClellan took the opportunity to regroup Porter's men with the main army south of the Chickahominy.

At this point McClellan yielded the initiative to Lee. With his line of communications cut to White House—his supply base on the York River—and with the James River open to the U.S. Navy, the Union commander decided to shift his base to Harrison's Landing on the south side of the peninsula. His rear areas had been particularly shaky since Confederate cavalry under Brig. Gen. J. E. B. Stuart had ridden completely around the Federal Army in a daring raid in early June. The intricate retreat to the James, which involved 90,000 men, the artillery train, 3,100 wagons, and 2,500 head of cattle, began on the night of June 27 and was accomplished by using two roads. Lee tried to hinder the movement but was held off by Federal rear guards at Savage Station on June 29 and at Frayser's Farm (Glendale) on the last day of the month.

By the first day of July McClellan had concentrated the Army of the Potomac on a commanding plateau at Malvern Hill, northwest of Harrison's Landing. The location was strong, with clear fields of fire to the front and the flanks secured by streams. Massed artillery could sweep all approaches and gunboats on the river were ready to provide fire support. The Confederates would have to attack by passing through broken and wooded terrain, traversing swampy ground, and ascending the hill. At first Lee felt McClellan's position was too strong to assault. Then, at 3 P.M. on July 1, when a shifting of Federal troops deceived him into thinking there was a general withdrawal, he changed his mind and attacked. Again staff work and control were poor. The assaults, which were all frontal, were delivered piecemeal by only part of the army against Union artillery, massed hub to hub, and supporting infantry. The Confederate formations were shattered because Lee failed to carry out the principle of mass. On the following day, the Army of the

47

Potomac fell back to Harrison's Landing and dug in. After reconnoitering McClellan's position, Lee ordered his exhausted men back to the Richmond lines for rest and reorganization.

The Peninsular Campaign cost the Federal Army some 15,849 men killed, wounded, and missing. The Confederates, who had done most of the attacking, lost 20,614. Improvement in the training and discipline of the two armies since the disorganized fight at Bull Run was notable. Also significant was the fact that higher commanders had not yet thoroughly mastered their jobs. Except in McClellan's defensive action at Malvern Hill, which was largely conducted by his corps commanders, neither side had been able to bring an entire army into co-ordinated action.

Second Manassas

Failure of the Union forces to take Richmond quickly forced President Lincoln to abandon the idea of exercising command over the Union armies in person. On July 11, 1862, he selected as new General in Chief Henry W. Halleck, who had won acclaim for the victories in the west. The President did not at once appoint a successor in the west, which was to suffer from divided command for a time. Lincoln wanted Halleck to direct the various Federal armies in close concert to take advantage of the North's superior strength. If all Federal armies co-ordinated their efforts, Lincoln reasoned, they could strike where the Confederacy was weak or force it to strengthen one army at the expense of another, and eventually they could wear the Confederacy down, destroy the various armies, and win the war.

Halleck turned out to be a disappointment. He never attempted to exercise field command or assume responsibility for strategic direction of the armies. But, acting more as military adviser to the President, he performed a valuable function by serving as a channel of communication between the Chief Executive and the field commanders. He adeptly translated the President's ideas into terms the generals could comprehend, and expressed the soldier's views in language that Mr. Lincoln could understand.

Shortly before Halleck's appointment, Lincoln also decided to consolidate the various Union forces in the Shenandoah Valley and other parts of western Virginia—some 45,000 men—under the victor at Island No. 10, Maj. Gen. John Pope. Pope immediately disenchanted his new command by pointing out that in the west the Federal armies were used to seeing the backs of their enemies. Pope's so-called Army of Virginia was ordered to divert pressure from McClellan on the peninsula. But Jackson had left the valley and Federal forces were scattered. On August 3, Halleck ordered McClellan to withdraw by water from the peninsula to Aquia Creek on the Potomac and to effect a speedy junction at Fredericksburg with Pope. Meanwhile Pope began posting the Army of Virginia along the Orange and Alexandria Railroad to the west of Fredericksburg.

Lee knew that his Army of Northern Virginia was in a dangerous position between Pope and McClellan, especially if the two were to unite. On July 13, he sent Jackson, with forces eventually totaling 24,000 men, to watch Pope. After an initial sparring action at Cedar Mountain on August 9, Jackson and Pope stood watching each other for nearly a week. Lee, knowing that McClellan was leaving Harrison's Landing, had departed Richmond with the remainder of the Army of Northern Virginia and joined Jackson at Gordonsville. The combined Confederate forces outnumbered Pope's, and Lee resolved to outflank and cut off the Army of Virginia before the whole of McClellan's force could be brought to bear.

A succession of captured orders enabled both Lee and Pope to learn the intentions of the other. Pope ascertained Lee's plan to trap him against the Rappahannock and withdrew to the north bank astride the railroad. Lee, learning that two corps from the Army of the Potomac would join Pope within days, acted quickly and boldly. He sent Jackson off on a wide turning movement through Thoroughfare Gap in the Bull Run Mountains around the northern flank of Pope's army and subsequently followed the same route with the divisions commanded by General Longstreet.

Pope took note of Jackson's move, but first assumed that it was pointed toward the Shenandoah Valley. Then Jackson, covering nearly sixty miles in two days, came in behind Pope at Manassas on August 26, destroyed his supply base there, and slipped away unmolested. Pope marched and counter-marched his forces for two days trying to find the elusive Confederates. At the same time the Union commander failed to take Lee's other forces into account. As a result he walked into Lee's trap on the site of the old battlefield of Manassas or Bull Run. Pope attacked Jackson, posted behind an abandoned railroad embankment, but again the attack consisted of a series of piecemeal frontal assaults which were repulsed with heavy casualties. By then Porter's V Corps from the Army of the Potomac had reached the field and was ordered to attack Jackson's right (south) flank. By this time also, Longstreet's column had burst through Thoroughfare Gap, and deploying on Jackson's right, it blocked Porter's move.

Next day, August 30, Pope renewed his attacks against Jackson, whom he thought to be retreating. Seizing the opportunity to catch the Federal columns in an exposed position, Lee sent Longstreet slashing along the Warrenton turnpike to hit Pope's flank. The Federal army soon retired from the field and Pope led it back to Washington, fighting an enveloping Confederate force at Chantilly on the way.

Lee, by great daring and rapid movement, and by virtue of having the Confederate forces unified under his command, had successfully defeated one formidable Union army in the presence of another even larger one. Halleck, as General in Chief, had not taken the field to co-ordinate Pope and McClellan, and Pope lost the campaign despite the advantage of interior lines.

President Lincoln, desiring to use McClellan's admitted talents for training and reorganizing the battered eastern armies, had become convinced that bitter personal feelings between McClellan and Pope prevented them from working effectively in the same theater. On September 5, Halleck, upon the President's order, dissolved the Army of Virginia and assigned its units to the Army of the Potomac. He sent Pope to a command in Minnesota. The Union authorities expected that McClellan would be able to devote several months to training and reorganization, but Lee dashed these hopes.

Lee Invades Maryland

Up to this point the Confederates in the east had been following defensive strategy, though tactically they frequently assumed the offensive. But Davis and Lee, for a complicated set of political and military reasons, determined to take the offensive and invade the North in co-ordination with Bragg's drive into Kentucky. Militarily, in the east, an invasion of Maryland would give Lee a chance to defeat or destroy the Army of the Potomac, uncovering such cities as Washington, Baltimore, and Philadelphia, and to cut Federal communications with the states to the west.

The Army of Northern Virginia, organized into two infantry commands (Longstreet's consisting of five divisions, and Jackson's of four divisions) plus Stuart's three brigades of cavalry, and the reserve artillery, numbered 55,000 effectives. Lee did not rest after Manassas but crossed the Potomac and encamped near Frederick, Maryland, from which he sent Jackson to capture an isolated Federal garrison at Harpers Ferry. The remainder of Lee's army then crossed South Mountain and headed for Hagerstown, about twenty-five miles northwest of Frederick, with Stuart's cavalry screening the right flank. In the meantime McClellan's rejuvenated Army of the Potomac, 90,000 men organized into six corps, marched northwest from Washington and reached Frederick on September 12.

At this time McClellan had a stroke of luck. Lee, in assigning missions to his command, had detached Maj. Gen. D. H. Hill's division from Jackson and attached it to Longstreet and had sent copies of his orders, which prescribed routes, objectives, and times of arrival, to Jackson, Longstreet, and Hill. But Jackson was not sure that Hill had received the order. He therefore made an additional copy of Lee's order and sent it to Hill. One of Hill's orders, wrapped around some cigars, was somehow left behind in an abandoned camp where it was picked up on September 13 by Union soldiers and rushed to McClellan. This windfall gave the Federal commander an unmatched opportunity to defeat Lee's scattered forces in detail if he pushed fast through the gaps. McClellan vacillated for sixteen hours. Lee, informed of the lost order, sent all available forces to hold the

51

gaps, so that it was nightfall on the 14th before McClellan fought his way across South Mountain.

Lee retreated to Sharpsburg on Antietam Creek where he turned to fight. Pinned between Antietam Creek and the Potomac with no room for maneuver, and still outnumbered since Jackson's force had yet to return to the main body after capturing Harpers Ferry, Lee relied on the advantage of interior lines and the boldness and the fighting ability of his men.

McClellan delayed his attack until September 17, when he launched an unco-ordinated series of assaults which drove back the Confederates in places but failed to break their line. Heavy fighting swelled across ripe fields and up through rocky glens that became known to history as the West Wood, the Cornfield, the East Wood, Bloody Lane, and Burnside's Bridge. One southerner remembered the attacking Union columns: "With flags flying and the long unfaltering lines rising and falling as they crossed the rolling fields, it looked as though nothing could stop them." But when the massed fire of field guns and small arms struck such human waves, a Union survivor recalled, it "was like a scythe running through our line."

McClellan, like too many leaders during the Civil War, could not bring himself to commit his reserve (the V Corps under Porter) at the strategy moment. Although adored by his men, as one of the veterans wrote after the war, he "never realized the metal that was in his grand Army of the Potomac." Jackson's last division arrived in time to head off the final assaults by Maj. Gen. Ambrose Burnside's corps, and at the end of the day Lee still held most of his line. Casualties were heavy. Of 70,000 Federal troops nearly 13,000 were killed, wounded, or missing, and the 40,000 or more Confederates engaged lost almost as many. Although Lee audaciously awaited new attacks on September 18, McClellan left him unmolested, and that night the Army of Northern Virginia withdrew across the Potomac.

Lincoln's Emancipation Proclamation

Antietam was tactically a draw, but the fact that Lee was forced to call off the invasion made it a strategic victory and gave President Lincoln an opportunity to strike at the Confederacy psychologically and economically by issuing the Emancipation Proclamation on September 22, 1862. Lincoln, while opposed to slavery and its extension to the western territories, was not an abolitionist. He had stated publicly that the war was being fought over union or secession, with the slavery question only incidental, and had earlier overruled several generals who were premature emancipators. But anticipating the total psychological warfare techniques of the twentieth century, he had for some time desired to free the slaves of the Confederate states in order to weaken their economies and to appeal to antislavery opinion in Europe. He had awaited the opportune moment that a Union victory would give him and decided that Antietam was suitable. Acting on his authority as Commander in Chief he issued the Proclamation which stated that all slaves in states or districts in rebellion against the United States on January 1, 1863, would be thenceforward and forever free. The Proclamation set no slaves free on the day it took effect. Negroes in the four slave states still in the Union were not touched, nor were the slaves in those Confederate areas that had been subjugated by Union bayonets. It had no immediate effect behind the Confederate lines, except to cause a good deal of excitement. But thereafter, as Union forces penetrated the South, the newly freed people deserted the farms and plantations and flocked to the colors.

Negroes had served in the Revolution, the War of 1812, and other early wars, but they had been barred from the Regular Army and, under the Militia Act of 1792, from the state militia. The Civil War marks their official debut in American military forces. Recruiting of Negroes began under the local auspices of Maj. Gen. David Hunter in the Department of the South as early as April 1862. There was a certain appeal to the idea that Negroes might assure their freedom by joining in the battle for it even if they served for lower pay in segregated units under white officers. On July 17, 1862, Congress authorized recruitment of Negroes while passing the antislavery Second Confiscation Act. The Emancipation Proclamation put the matter in a new light, and on May 22, 1863, the War Department established a Bureau of Colored Troops, another innovation of the Civil War since it was an example of Federal volunteer formations without official ties to specific states (others being the various U.S. sharp-shooter regiments and the invalid Veteran Reserve Corps). By the end of the war 100,000 Negroes were enrolled as U.S. Volunteers. Many other Negroes served in state units, elsewhere in the armed forces, and as laborers for the Union Army.

Fiasco at Fredericksburg

After Antietam both armies returned to face each other in Virginia, Lee situated near Culpeper and McClellan at Warrenton. But McClellan's slowness, his failure to accomplish more at Antietam, and perhaps his rather arrogant habit of offering gratuitous political advice to his superiors, coupled with the intense anti-McClellan views of the joint Congressional Committee on the Conduct of the War, convinced Lincoln that he could retain him in command no longer. On November 7 Lincoln replaced him with Burnside, who had won distinction in operations that gained control of ports on the North Carolina coast and who had led the IX Corps at Antietam. Burnside accepted the post with reluctance.

Burnside decided to march rapidly to Fredericksburg and then advance along the railroad line to Richmond before Lee could intercept him. *(Map 7)* Such a move by the army—now 120,000 strong—would cut Lee off from his main base. Burnside's advance elements reached the north bank of the Rappahannock on November 17, well ahead of Lee. But a series of minor failures delayed the completion of ponton bridges, and Lee moved his army to high ground on the south side of the river before the Federal forces could cross. Lee's situation resembled McClellan's position at Malvern Hill which had proved the folly of frontal assaults against combined artillery and infantry strongpoints. But Burnside thought the sheer weight of numbers could smash through the Confederates.

To achieve greater ease of tactical control, Burnside had created three headquarters higher than corps—the Right, Center, and Left Grand Divisions under Maj. Gens. Edwin V. Sumner, Joseph Hooker, and William B. Franklin, respectively—

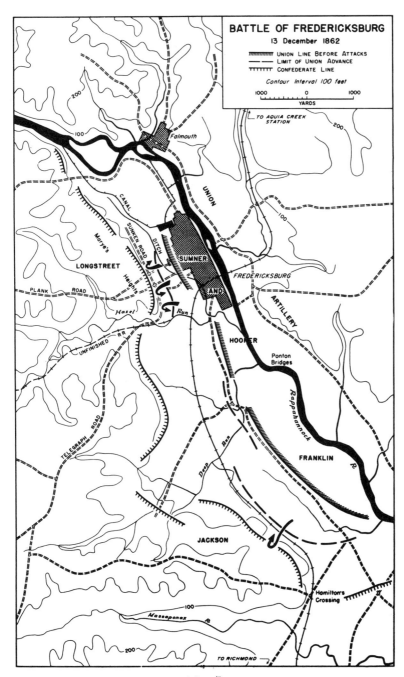

BATTLE OF FREDERICKSBURG
13 December 1862

mmmmmm UNION LINE BEFORE ATTACKS
— — — LIMIT OF UNION ADVANCE
ттттттт CONFEDERATE LINE

Contour Interval 100 feet

1000   0   1000
YARDS

TO AQUIA CREEK
STATION

Falmouth

UNION

CANAL

SUNKEN ROAD

DITCH

Marye's

LONGSTREET

SUMNER

Heights

PLANK   ROAD

FREDERICKSBURG

Hazel

Run

ARTILLERY

UNFINISHED   RR

HOOKER

Ponton
Bridges

TELEGRAPH   ROAD

Deep   Run

Rappahannock   R.

FRANKLIN

JACKSON

Hamilton's
Crossing

100

Massaponax   R.

200

TO RICHMOND

Map 7

with two corps plus cavalry assigned to each grand division. Burnside originally planned to make the main thrust by Center and Left Grand Divisions against Jackson's positions on a long, low-wooded ridge southeast of the town. The Right Grand Division would cross three ponton bridges at Fredericksburg and attack Marye's Heights, a steep eminence about one mile from the river where Longstreet's men were posted. On the morning of December 13, he weakened the attack on the left, feeling that under cover of 147 heavy siege and field guns on the heights on the Union side of the river much could be achieved by a better-balanced attack along the whole line.

Burnside's engineers had begun laying the bridges as early as December 11. But harassment from Confederate sharpshooters complicated the operation, and it was not until the next day that all the assault units were over the river. After an artillery duel on the morning of the 13th, fog lifted to reveal dense Union columns moving forward to the attack. Part of the Left Grand Division, finding a weakness in Jackson's line, drove in to seize the ridge, but as Burnside had weakened this part of the assault the Federals were not able to hold against Confederate counterattacks. On the right, the troops had to cross a mile of open ground to reach Marye's Heights, traverse a drainage canal, and face a fusillade of fire from the infamous sunken road and stone wall behind which Longstreet had placed four ranks of riflemen. In a series of assaults the Union soldiers pushed to the stone wall but no farther. As a demonstration of valor the effort was exemplary; as a demonstration of tactical skill it was tragic. Lee, observing the shattered attackers, commented: "It is well that war is so terrible—we should grow too fond of it."

The Army of the Potomac lost 12,000 men at Fredericksburg while the Army of Northern Virginia suffered only 5,300 casualties. Burnside planned to renew the attack on the following day and Jackson, whose enthusiasm in battle sometimes approached the point of frenzy, suggested that the Confederates strip off their clothes for better identification and strike the Army of the Potomac in a night attack. But Lee knew of Burnside's plans from a captured order and vetoed the scheme. When the Federal corps commanders talked Burnside out of renewing the attack, both armies settled into winter quarters facing each other across the Rappahannock. Fredericksburg, a disastrous defeat, was otherwise noteworthy for the U.S. Army in that the telegraph first saw extensive battlefield use, linking headquarters with forward batteries during the action—a forerunner of twentieth century battlefield communications.

West of the Mississippi

If the major fighting of the Civil War occurred in the "older" populated sections of the United States, the youthful area of the American frontier across the Mississippi saw its share of action also. Missouri and Kansas, and indeed the distant New Mexico Territory (all areas involved in the root causes for the conflict), were touched by the Civil War.

The Southwest was a particularly rich plum, for as one Confederate commander observed: "The vast mineral resources of Arizona, in addition to its affording an outlet to the Pacific, makes its acquisition a matter of some importance to our Govt." Also it was assumed that Indians and the Mormons in Utah would readily accept allegiance to almost any government other than that in Washington.

It was with these motives in mind that early in 1862 Confederate forces moved up the Rio Grande valley and proceeded to establish that part of New Mexico Territory north of the 34th parallel as the Confederate territory of Arizona. Under Brig. Gen. Henry H. Sibley, inventor of a famous tent bearing his name, the Confederates successfully swept all the way to Santa Fe, capital of New Mexico, bypassing several Union garrisons on the way. But Sibley was dangerously overextended, and Federal troops, reinforced by Colorado volunteers, surprised the advancing Confederates in Apache Canyon on March 26 and 28, as they sought to capture the largest Union garrison in the territory at Fort Union.

One of the bypassed Federal columns under Col. Edward R. S. Canby from Fort Craig meanwhile joined the Fort Union troops against the Confederates. Unable to capture the Union posts, unable to resupply his forces, and learning of yet a third

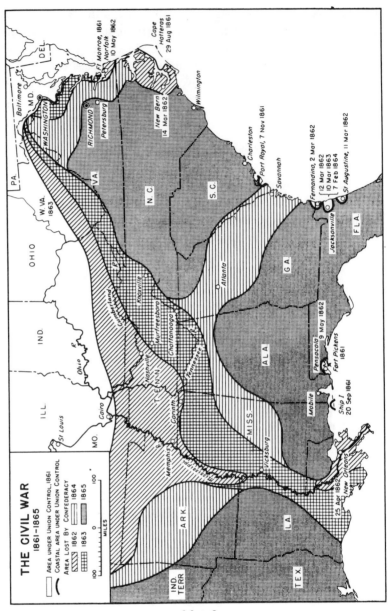

Map 8

Federal column converging on him from California, Sibley
began a determined retreat down the Rio Grande valley. By

58

May he was back in Texas and the Confederate invasion of New Mexico was ended. The fighting, on a small scale by eastern standards, provided valuable training for Federal troops involved later in Indian wars in this area. Indeed, while the Confederate dream of a new territory and an outlet to the Pacific was shattered by 1862, Indian leaders in the mountain territories saw an opportunity to reconquer lost land while the white men were otherwise preoccupied. In 1863 and 1864 both Federal and Confederate troops in the southwest were kept busy fighting hostile tribes. *(Map 8)*

In Missouri and Arkansas, fighting had erupted on a large scale by the early spring of 1862. Federal authorities had retained a precarious hold over Missouri when Maj. Gen. Samuel R. Curtis with 11,000 men chased disorganized Confederates back into Arkansas. But under General Van Dorn and Maj. Gen. Sterling Price, the Confederates regrouped and embarked upon a counteroffensive which only ended at Pea Ridge on March 7 and 8. Here Van Dorn executed a double envelopment as half his army stole behind Pea Ridge, marched around three-fourths of Curtis' force, and struck Curtis' left rear near Elkhorn Tavern while the other half attacked his right rear. But in so doing the Confederates uncovered their own line of communications and Curtis' troops turned around and fought off the attacks from the rear. After initial success, Van Dorn and Price were unable to continue the contest and withdrew. For three more years guerrilla warfare would ravage Missouri, but the Union grip on the state was secure.

The year 1862, which began with impressive Union victories in the west, ended in bitter frustration in the east. Ten full-scale and costly battles had been fought, but no decisive victory had yet been scored by the forces of the Union. The Federals had broken the great Confederate counteroffensives in the fall only to see their hopes fade with the advent of winter. The Union war machine had lost its earlier momentum.

CHAPTER 3

1863

At the beginning of 1863 the Confederacy seemed to have a fair chance of ultimate success on the battlefield. But during this year three great campaigns would take place that would shape the outcome of the war in favor of the North. One would see the final solution to the control of the Mississippi River. A second, concurrent with the first, would break the back of any Confederate hopes for success by invasion of the North and recognition abroad. The third, slow and uncertain in its first phases, would result eventually in Union control of the strategic gateway to the 'South Atlantic region of the Confederacy—the last great stronghold of secession and the area in which the internecine conflict would come of age as modern total war.

Confusion Over Clearing the Mississippi

When Halleck went east in September 1862 to become General in Chief, his splendid army was divided between Grant and Buell. Grant, with over 60,000 men, remained in western Tennessee guarding communication lines. Buell's army of 56,000, after containing Bragg's invasion of Kentucky, had been taken over by Rosecrans, whose hard-won victory at Murfreesboro at the end of 1862 nevertheless immobilized the Army of the Cumberland for nearly half a year. To the west, only the posts at Vicksburg and Port Hudson prevented the Union from controlling the entire length of the Mississippi and splitting the Confederacy in two. Naval expeditions, under Capt. David G. Farragut, supported by the army, tried to seize

Vicksburg in May and again in July 1862, but the Confederates easily repulsed the attempts. In the autumn Grant pressed Halleck to let him get on with the campaign down the Mississippi and finally received the response: "Fight the enemy where you please." But while Halleck and Grant were planning to move against Vicksburg by water and land, Lincoln and Stanton also outlined a similar move, but without consulting the military leaders.

The Chief Executive had long seen the importance of controlling the Mississippi, and in the fall of 1862 he and the Secretary of War prepared plans for a simultaneous advance northward from New Orleans and southward from Tennessee. Somewhat vague orders were drawn up giving command of the northbound expedition to Maj. Gen. Nathaniel Banks, who had replaced Butler as commander of the Department of the Gulf. Command of the southbound expedition was to go to Maj. Gen. John A. McClernand. Both officers were relatively untried, unstable, volunteer officers and politicians who often dabbled in intrigue in order to gain favors. Further, McClernand was to operate within Grant's department but independently of him. When Halleck found out about the Lincoln-Stanton plan, he persuaded the President to put Grant in command of the southbound expedition and to make McClernand one of his subordinates.

Grant's Campaign Against Vicksburg

Grant first tried a combined land and water expedition against Vicksburg in December 1862–January 1863. He sent Maj. Gen. William T. Sherman down river from Memphis, but the Confederates under Van Dorn and Forrest raided and cut the 200-mile-long line of communications. Sherman himself bogged down before Vicksburg, and Grant, perhaps also wishing to keep close rein on McClernand, who ranked Sherman, then determined on a river expedition which he would lead in person. Late in January Grant arrived before Vicksburg. He had upwards of 45,000 men, organized into three corps, the XIII Corps under McClernand, the XV Corps under Sherman, and

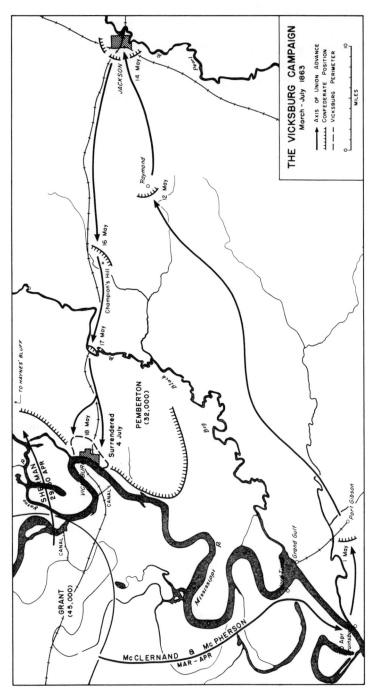

Map 9

Maj. Gen. James B. McPherson's XVII Corps. During the ensuing campaign Grant received two more corps as reinforcements to bring his total strength to 75,000 men.

Vicksburg had almost a perfect location for defense. *(Map 9)* At that point on the river, bluffs rose as high as 250 feet above the water and extended for about 100 miles from north to south. North of Vicksburg lay the Yazoo River and its delta, a gloomy stretch of watery, swampy bottom land extending 175 miles from north to south, 60 miles from east to west. The ground immediately south of Vicksburg was almost as swampy and impassable. The Confederates had fortified the bluffs from Haynes' Bluff on the Yazoo, some 10 miles above Vicksburg, to Grand Gulf at the mouth of the Big Black River about 40 miles below. Vicksburg could not be assaulted from the river, and sailing past it was extremely hazardous. The river formed a great U here, and Vicksburg's guns threatened any craft that tried to run by. For the Union troops to attack successfully, they would have to get to the high, dry ground east of town. This would put them in Confederate territory between two enemy forces. Lt. Gen. John C. Pemberton commanded some 30,000 men in Vicksburg, while the Confederate area commander, General Joseph E. Johnston (now recovered from his wound at Fair Oaks), concentrated the other scattered Confederate forces in Mississippi at Jackson, the state capital, 40 miles east of Vicksburg.

During late winter and early spring, with the rains falling, the streams high, and the roads at their wettest and muddiest, overland movement was impossible. Primarily to placate discontented politicians and a critical press, Grant made four attempts to reach high ground east of Vicksburg. All four were unsuccessful, foiled either by Confederate resistance or by natural obstacles. One of the more spectacular efforts was digging canals. These projects had as their objective the clearing of an approach by which troops could sail to a point near the high ground without being fired on by Vicksburg's guns, and all failed. That Grant kept on trying in the face of such discouragement is a tribute to his dogged persistence, and that Lincoln supported him is a tribute to his confidence in the general. The trouble was that Grant had been on the river for two months,

63

and by early spring, Vicksburg was no nearer falling than when he came.

On April 4 in a letter to Halleck, Grant divulged his latest plan to capture Vicksburg. Working closely with the local naval commander, Flag Officer David D. Porter, Grant evolved a stroke of great boldness. He decided to use part of his force above Vicksburg to divert the Confederates while the main body marched southward on the west side of the Mississippi, crossed to the east bank, and with only five days' rations struck inland to live off a hostile country without a line of supply or retreat. As he told Sherman, the Union troops would carry "what rations of hard bread, coffee, and salt we can and make the country furnish the balance." Porter's gunboats and other craft, which up to now were on the river north of Vicksburg, were to run past the batteries during darkness and then ferry the troops over the river. Sherman thought the campaign too risky, but the events of the next two months were to prove him wrong.

While Sherman demonstrated near Vicksburg in March, McClernand's and McPherson's corps started their advance south. The rains let up in April, the waters receded slightly, and overland movement became somewhat easier. On the night of April 16 Porter led his river fleet past Vicksburg, whose guns, once the move was discovered, lit up the black night with an eerie bombardment. All but one transport made it safely, and starting on April 30, Porter's craft ferried the troops eastward over the river at Bruinsburg below Grand Gulf. The final march against Vicksburg was ready to begin.

At this time the Confederates had more troops in the vicinity than Grant had but never could make proper use of them. Grant's swift move had bewildered Pemberton. Then too, just before marching downstream, Grant had ordered a brigade of cavalry to come down from the Tennessee border, riding between the parallel north-south railroad lines of the Mississippi Central and Mobile and Ohio. Led by Col. Benjamin H. Grierson, this force sliced the length of the state, cutting railroads, fighting detachments of Confederate cavalry, and finally reaching Union lines at Baton Rouge, Louisiana. Most important, for the few days that counted most, it drew

Pemberton's attention away from Grant and kept the Confederate general from discerning the Union's objectives.

Once more divided counsel hampered co-ordination of Confederate strategy. Johnston had been sent west by Davis to take over-all command, an imposing task, for Pemberton's army in Mississippi and Bragg's in Tennessee were widely separated. Things were further confused by Davis' directive to Pemberton to hold Vicksburg at all costs while Johnston recognized the potential trap and ordered him to move directly against Grant. In such a situation Pemberton could do little that was right. He tried to defend too wide an area; he had not concentrated but dispersed his forces at Vicksburg, the Big Black River, and along the railroad line to Jackson, where Johnston was gathering more troops.

After Grant had captured Port Gibson on May 1, and Sherman's corps had rejoined the main force, the Union commander decided that he must defeat Johnston before turning on Vicksburg. He moved northeastward and fought his way into Raymond on May 12, a move which put him squarely between Johnston and Pemberton and in a position to cut the Confederate line of communications. Next day Sherman and McPherson marched against the city of Jackson, with McClernand following in reserve, ready to hold off Pemberton. The leading corps took Jackson on May 14 and drove its garrison eastward. While Sherman occupied the state capital to fend off Johnston, the other two corps turned west against Pemberton and Vicksburg. Pemberton tried too late to catch Grant in open country. He suffered severe defeats at Champion's Hill (May 16) and Black River Bridge (May 17) and was shut up in Vicksburg. In eighteen days Grant's army had marched 200 miles, had won four victories, and had finally secured the high ground along the Yazoo River that had been the goal of all the winter's fruitless campaigning.

Grant assaulted the Vicksburg lines on May 18 and 22, but as Sherman noted of the attacks: "The heads of columns have been swept away as chaff from the hand on a windy day." The only recourse now was a siege. Grant settled down, and removed McClernand from command after the attack of May 22 during which the corps commander sent a misleading report, then later slighted the efforts of the other corps and publicly criticized the army commander. Grant replaced him with Maj. Gen. Edward O. C. Ord, and ordered the army to implant batteries and dig trenches around the city.

The rest was now a matter of time, as Sherman easily kept Johnston away and the Federals advanced their siegeworks toward the Confederate fortifications. Food became scarce and the troops and civilians inside Vicksburg were soon reduced to eating mules and horses. Shells pounded the city, and the Federal lines were drawn so tight that one Confederate soldier admitted that "a cat could not have crept out of Vicksburg without being discovered." The front lines were so close that the Federals threw primitive hand grenades into the Confederate works. By July 1 the Union troops had completed their approaches and were ready for another assault. But Vicksburg was starving and Pemberton asked for terms. Grant offered to parole all prisoners, and the city surrendered on Independence Day. Since Grant was out of telegraphic contact with Washington, the news reached the President via naval channels on July 7, the day before General Banks' 15,000-man army, having advanced up river from New Orleans, captured Port Hudson. The whole river was now repossessed by the Union, the Confederacy sliced in two. Once more Grant had removed an entire Confederate army from the war—40,000 men—losing only one-tenth that number in the process.

Hooker Crosses the Rappahannock

Events in the western theater in the spring and early summer of 1863 were impressive. Those in the east during the same period were fewer in number but equally dramatic. After the battle of Fredericksburg, Burnside's Army of the Potomac went into winter quarters on the north bank of the Rappahannock, while the main body of Lee's Army of Northern Virginia held Fredericksburg and guarded the railway line to Richmond. During January, Burnside's subordinates intrigued against him and went out of channels to present their grievances to Congress

U.S. Army   C. S. Army

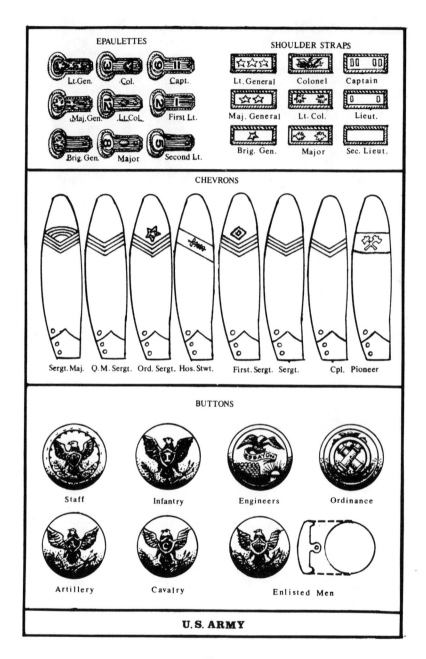

EPAULETTES

Lt.Gen. Col. Capt.

Maj.Gen. Lt.Col. First Lt.

Brig. Gen. Major Second Lt.

SHOULDER STRAPS

Lt. General Colonel Captain

Maj. General Lt. Col. Lieut.

Brig. Gen. Major Sec. Lieut.

CHEVRONS

Sergt. Maj. Q.M. Sergt. Ord. Sergt. Hos. Stwt. First. Sergt. Sergt. Cpl. Pioneer

BUTTONS

Staff Infantry Engineers Ordinance

Artillery Cavalry Enlisted Men

U.S. ARMY

68

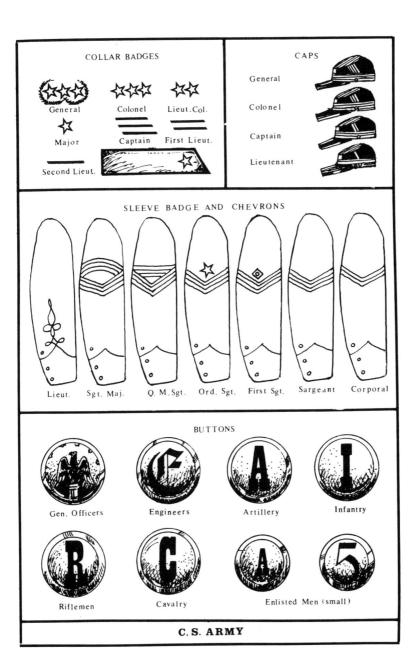

COLLAR BADGES

General
Colonel
Lieut.Col.
Major
Captain
First Lieut.
Second Lieut.

CAPS

General
Colonel
Captain
Lieutenant

SLEEVE BADGE AND CHEVRONS

Lieut.   Sgt. Maj.   Q. M. Sgt.   Ord. Sgt.   First Sgt.   Sargeant   Corporal

BUTTONS

Gen. Officers   Engineers   Artillery   Infantry

Riflemen   Cavalry   Enlisted Men (small)

C.S. ARMY

69

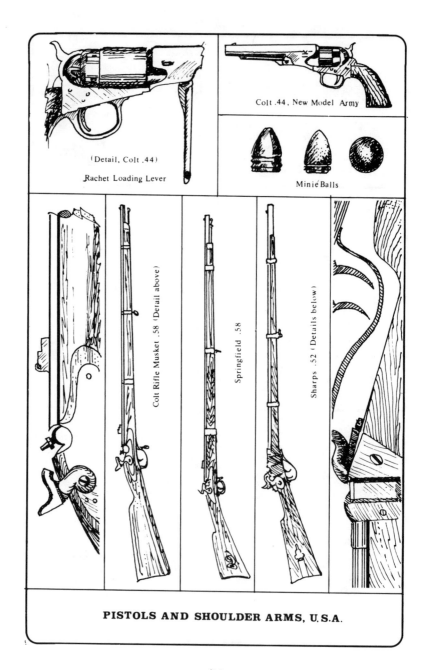

(Detail, Colt .44)

Rachet Loading Lever

Colt .44, New Model Army

Minié Balls

Colt Rifle Musket .58 (Detail above)

Springfield .58

Sharps .52 (Details below)

PISTOLS AND SHOULDER ARMS, U.S.A.

70

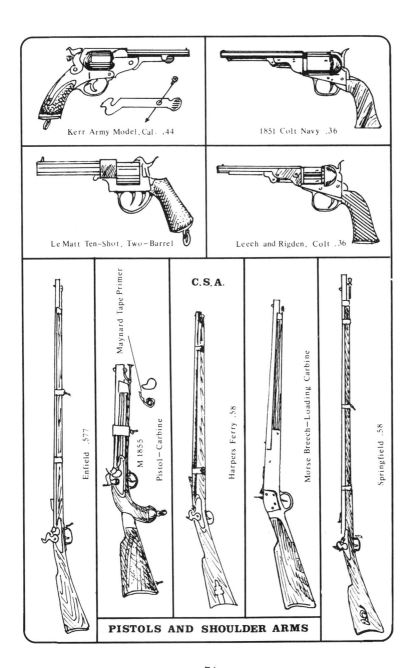

Kerr Army Model, Cal. .44

1851 Colt Navy .36

Le Matt Ten-Shot, Two-Barrel

Leech and Rigden, Colt .36

C.S.A.

Enfield .577

Maynard Tape Primer

M 1855 Pistol—Carbine

Harpers Ferry .58

Morse Breech—Loading Carbine

Springfield .58

PISTOLS AND SHOULDER ARMS

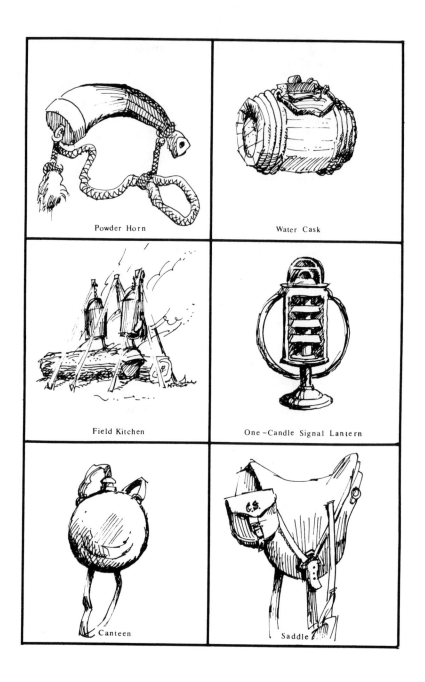

Powder Horn

Water Cask

Field Kitchen

One-Candle Signal Lantern

Canteen

Saddle

72

and the President. When Burnside heard of this development, he asked that either he or most of the subordinate general officers be removed. The President accepted the first alternative, and on January 25, 1863, replaced Burnside with Maj. Gen. Joseph Hooker. The new commander had won the sobriquet of "Fighting Joe" for his intrepid reputation as a division and corps commander. He was highly favored in Washington, but in appointing him the President took the occasion to write a fatherly letter in which he warned the general against rashness and overambition, reproached him for plotting against Burnside, and concluded by asking for victories.

Under Hooker's able administration, discipline and training improved. Morale, which had fallen after Fredericksburg, rose as Hooker regularized the furlough system and improved the flow of rations and other supplies to his front-line troops. Abolishing Burnside's grand divisions Hooker returned to the orthodox corps, of which he had seven, each numbering about 15,000 men. One of Hooker's most effective innovations was the introduction of distinctive corps and division insignia. He also took a long step toward improving the cavalry arm of the army, which up to this time had been assigned many diverse duties and was split up into small detachments. Hooker regarded cavalry as a combat arm of full stature, and he concentrated his units into a cavalry corps of three divisions under Brig. Gen. George Stoneman. On the other hand Hooker made a costly mistake in decentralizing tactical control of his artillery to his corps commanders. As a result Union artillery would not be properly massed in the coming action at Chancellorsville.

Hooker had no intention of repeating Burnside's tragic frontal assault at Fredericksburg. With a strength approaching 134,000 men, Hooker planned a double envelopment which would place strong Union forces on each of Lee's flanks. *(Map 10)* He ordered three of his infantry corps to move secretly up the Rappahannock and ford the stream, while two more corps, having conspicuously remained opposite Fredericksburg, were to strike across the old battlefield there. Two more corps were in reserve. The cavalry corps, less one division which was to screen the move up river, was to raid far behind Lee's rear to divert him. Hooker's plan was superb; his execution faulty. The three corps

73

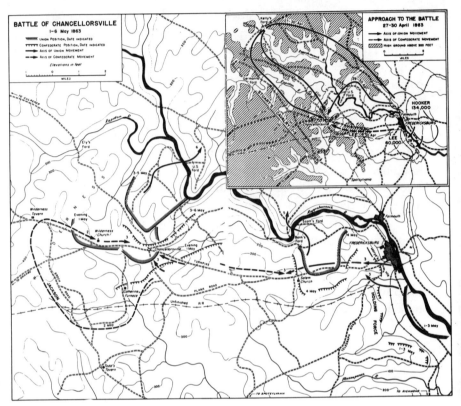

Map 10

moved quickly up the river and by the end of April had crossed
and advanced to the principal road junction of Chancellorsville.
They were now in the so-called "Wilderness," a low, flat,
confusing area of scrub timber and narrow dirt roads in which
movement and visibility were extremely limited. Maj. Gen.
John Sedgwick crossed the Rappahannock at Fredericksburg on
the 29th, and the two remaining corps moved to within
supporting distance of Hooker at Chancellorsville. So far
everything had gone according to plan, except that Stoneman's
diversion had failed to bother Lee. One of Stuart's brigades kept
Stoneman under surveillance while the main body of cavalry

shadowed Hooker so effectively that the southern commander knew every move made by the Union army. By the morning of April 30, Lee was aware of what was afoot and knew that he was threatened by double envelopment. Already Hooker was sending his columns eastward toward the back door to Fredericksburg. A less bold and resolute man than Lee would have retreated southward at once, and with such ample justification that only the captious would have found fault. But the southern general, his army numbering only 60,000, used the principles of the offensive, maneuver, economy of force, and surprise to compensate for his inferior numbers. Instead of retreating, he left a part of his army to hold the heights at Fredericksburg and started west for Chancellorsville with the main body.

Chancellorsville: Lee's Finest Battle

When Lee began to move, Hooker simply lost his courage. Over protests of his corps commanders, he ordered the troops back into defensive positions around Chancellorsville. The Federals established a line in the forest, felled trees for an abatis, and constructed earth-and-log breastworks. Their position faced generally south, anchored on the Rappahannock on the east; but in the west it was weak, unsupported, and hanging in the air. Lee brought his main body up and on May 1 made contact with Hooker's strong left. That day Stuart's cavalry discovered Hooker's vulnerable right flank and promptly reported the intelligence to Lee. Conferring that night with Stonewall Jackson, Lee made another bold decision. Facing an army much greater than his own, he decided to divide his forces and further envelop the envelopers. Accordingly, Lee committed about 17,000 men against Hooker's left to hold it in place while Jackson with some 26,000 men made a wide 15-mile swing to get beyond the right flank. At first glance Lee's decision might appear a violation of the principles of mass and concentration, but while Lee's two forces were initially separated their common objective was the Army of the Potomac, and their ultimate routes converged on a common center.

Jackson's force, in a 10-mile-long column, moved out at

daybreak of May 2, marching southwest first, then swinging northwest to get into position. The Federals noted that something was happening off to the south but were unable to penetrate the defensive screen; Hooker soon began to think Lee was actually retreating. In late afternoon Jackson turned onto the Orange turnpike near Wilderness Tavern. This move put him west of Hooker's right flank, and since the woods thinned out a little at this point it was possible to form a line of battle. Because time was running short and the hour of the day was late, Jackson deployed in column of divisions, with each division formed with brigades abreast, the same kind of confusing formation Johnston had used at Shiloh. Shortly after 5 P.M. Jackson's leading division, shrieking the "rebel yell" and driving startled rabbits and deer before it, came charging out of the woods, rolling up Maj. Gen. Oliver O. Howard's XI Corps in wild rout. The Confederates pressed forward, but fresh Union troops, disorganization of his own men, and oncoming darkness stymied the impatient Jackson. While searching for a road that would permit him to cut off Hooker from United States Ford across the Rappahannock, Jackson fell prey to a mistaken ambush by his own men. The Confederate leader was wounded and died eight days later. During the night of May 2, Stuart, Jackson's successor as corps commander, re-formed his lines. Against Stuart's right, Hooker launched local counterattacks which at first gained some success, but the next morning withdrew his whole line. Once more Hooker yielded the initiative at the moment he had a strong force between Lee's two divided and weaker forces.

Stuart renewed the attack during the morning as Hooker pulled his line back. Hooker was knocked unconscious when a shell struck the pillar of the Chancellor house against which he was leaning. Until the end of the battle he was dazed and incapable of exercising effective command, but he did not relinquish it nor would the army's medical director declare him unfit. Meanwhile Sedgwick, who shortly after Jackson's attack had received orders to proceed through Fredericksburg to Chancellorsville, had assaulted Marye's Heights. He carried it about noon on May 3, but the next day Lee once more divided his command, leaving Stuart with 25,000 to guard Hooker, and moved himself with 21,000 to thwart Sedgwick. In a sharp action at Salem Church Lee forced the Federals off the road and northward over the Rappahannock. Lee now made ready for a full-scale assault against the Army of the Potomac huddled with its back against the river on May 6, but Hooker ordered retirement to the north bank before the attack. Confederate losses were approximately 13,000; Federal losses, 17,000. But Lee lost far more with the death of Jackson. Actually, Lee's brilliant and daring maneuvers had defeated only one man—Hooker— and in no other action of the war did moral superiority of one general over the other stand out so clearly as a decisive factor in battle. Chancellorsville exemplified Napoleon's maxim: "The General is the head, the whole of the army."

Hooker was a talented tactical commander with a good reputation. But in spite of Lincoln's injunction, "This time, put in all your men," he allowed nearly one-third of his army to stand idle during the heaviest fighting. Here again was a general who could effectively lead a body of troops under his own eyes but could not use maps and reports to evaluate and control situations that were beyond his range of vision. Hooker, not the Army of the Potomac, lost the battle of Chancellorsville. Yet for the victors, Chancellorsville was a hollow triumph. It was dazzling, a set piece for the instruction of students of the military art ever since, but it had been inconclusive, winning glory and little more. It left government and army on both sides with precisely the problems they had faced before the campaign began.

Lee's Second Invasion of the North

By 1863 the war had entered what Sherman called its professional phase. The troops were well trained and had ample combat experience. Officers had generally mastered their jobs and were deploying their forces fairly skillfully in accordance with the day's tactical principles. Furthermore, the increased range and accuracy of weapons, together with the nature of the terrain, had induced some alterations in tactics, alterations which were embodied in a revised infantry manual published in

1863. Thus, by the third year of the war, battles had begun to take on certain definite characteristics. The battle of Gettysburg was a case in point.

Gettysburg was, first of all, an act of fate—a three-day holocaust, largely unplanned and uncontrollable. Like the war itself, it sprang from decisions that men under pressure made in the light of imperfect knowledge. It would someday symbolize the war with all the blunders and heroism, hopes and delusions, combativeness and blinding devotion of the Amercan man in arms of that period. With its enormous destruction, tactical maneuvers, and use of weapons, Gettysburg was one of the most dramatic and most typical of the 2,000-odd land engagements of the Civil War.

After the great victory at Chancellorsville, the Confederate cause in the eastern theater looked exceptionally bright. If 60,000 men could beat 134,000, then the Confederacy's inferiority in manpower was surely offset by superior generalship and skill at arms. Vicksburg was not yet under siege, although Grant had ferried his army over to the east bank of the Mississippi. If Davis and Lee were overly optimistic, they could hardly be blamed. Both men favored another invasion of the North for much the same political and military reasons that led to invasion in 1862. Longstreet, on the other hand, was concerned over the Federal threats in the west. He proposed going on the defensive in Virginia and advised taking advantage of the Confederacy's railroads and interior lines to send part of the Army of Northern Virginia to Tennessee to relieve pressure on Vicksburg. But he was overruled and Lee made ready to move into Pennsylvania. By this time Union strategy in the east was clearly defined: to continue operations against Confederate seaports—an attempt to seize Fort Sumter on April 7 had failed—and to destroy Lee's army. President Lincoln's orders made clear that the destruction of the Army of Northern Virginia was the major objective of the Army of the Potomac. Richmond was only incidental.

On June 30, 1863, the Army of the Potomac numbered 115,256 officers and enlisted men, with 362 guns. It consisted of 51 infantry brigades organized into 19 divisions, which in turn formed seven infantry corps. The cavalry corps had three divisions. The field artillery, 67 batteries, was assigned by brigades to the corps, except for army reserve artillery. The Army of Northern Virginia, numbering 76,224 men and 272 guns in late May, comprised three infantry corps, each led by a lieutenant general, and Stuart's cavalry division. (The Confederacy was much more generous with rank than was the U.S. Army.) In each corps were three divisions, and most divisions had four brigades. Of the 15 field artillery battalions of four batteries each, five battalions were attached to each corps under command of the corps' artillery chiefs.

In early June Lee began moving his units away from Fredericksburg. In his advance he used the Shenandoah and Cumberland Valleys, for by holding the east-west mountain passes he could readily cover his approach route and line of communications. Hooker got wind of the move; he noted the weakening of the Fredericksburg defenses, and on June 9 his cavalry, commanded by Brig. Gen. Alfred Pleasonton, surprised Stuart at Brandy Station, Virginia. Here on an open plain was fought one of the few mounted, saber-swinging, cut-and-thrust cavalry combats of the Civil War. Up to now the Confederate cavalry had been superior, but at Brandy Station the Union horsemen "came of age," and Stuart was lucky to hold his position.

When the Federals learned that Confederate infantrymen were west of the Blue Ridge heading north, Hooker started to move to protect Washington and Baltimore and to attempt to destroy Lee. Earlier, Lincoln had vetoed Hooker's proposal to seize Richmond while Lee went north. As the Army of Northern Virginia moved through the valleys and deployed into Pennsylvania behind cavalry screens, the Army of the Potomac moved north on a broad front to the east, crossing the Potomac on June 25 and 26. Lee, forced to disperse by the lack of supplies, had extended his infantry columns from McConnellsburg and Chambersburg on the west to Carlisle in the north and York on the east.

After Brandy Station, and some sharp clashes in the mountain passes, Stuart set forth on another dramatic ride around the Union army. With only vague instructions and acting largely on his own initiative, he proved of little use to Lee. It was only on the afternoon of July 2 with his troopers so weary that they were almost falling from their saddles, that Stuart rejoined Lee in the vicinity of Gettysburg, too late to have an important influence on the battle. His absence had deprived Lee of prompt, accurate information about the Army of the Potomac. When Lee learned from Longstreet on June 28 that Hooker's men were north of the Potomac, he ordered his widespread units to concentrate at once between Gettysburg and Cashtown.

After Chancellorsville, Lincoln, though advised to drop Hooker, had kept him in command of the Army of the Potomac on the theory that he would not throw away a gun because it has misfired once. But Hooker soon became embroiled with Halleck and requested his own relief. He was replaced by a corps commander, Maj. Gen. George G. Meade, who before dawn on June 28 received word of his promotion and the accompanying problems inherent in assuming command of a great army while it was moving toward the enemy. Meade, who was to command the Army of the Potomac for the rest of the war, started north on a broad front at once but within two days decided to fight a defensive action in Maryland and issued orders to that effect. Not all his commanders received the order, and events overruled him.

Gettysburg

Outposts of both armies clashed during the afternoon of June 30 near the quiet little Pennsylvania market town of Gettysburg. The terrain in the area included rolling hills and broad shallow valleys. Gettysburg was the junction of twelve roads that led to Harrisburg, Philadelphia, Baltimore, Washington, and the mountain passes to the west which were controlled by Lee. The rest was inevitable; the local commanders sent reports and recommendations to their superiors, who relayed them upward, so that both armies, still widely dispersed, started moving toward Gettysburg. *(Map 11)*

On July 1, Union cavalrymen fought a dismounted delaying action against advance troops of Lt. Gen. Ambrose P. Hill's corps northwest of town. By this stage of the war cavalrymen,

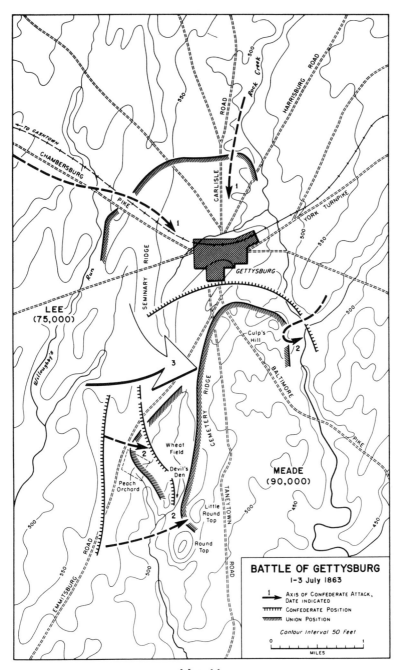

TO CASHTOWN

CHAMBERSBURG

PIKE

CARLISLE ROAD

Rock Creek

HARRISBURG ROAD

YORK TURNPIKE

SEMINARY RIDGE

Willoughby's Run

GETTYSBURG

LEE
(75,000)

Culp's
Hill

CEMETERY RIDGE

BALTIMORE PIKE

Wheat
Field

Devil's
Den

Peach
Orchard

Little
Round
Top

TANEYTOWN ROAD

MEADE
(90,000)

Round
Top

EMMITSBURG ROAD

BATTLE OF GETTYSBURG
1-3 July 1863

→1   Axis of Confederate Attack,
Date indicated

⊤⊤⊤⊤⊤   Confederate Position

⊥⊥⊥⊥⊥   Union Position

Contour Interval 50 Feet

0   1
MILES

Map 11

armed with saber, pistol, and breech-loading carbine, were often deployed as mounted infantrymen, riding to battle but fighting on foot. The range and accuracy of the infantry's rifled muskets made it next to impossible for mounted men to attack foot soldiers in position. With their superior speed and mobility, cavalrymen, as witnessed in the Gettysburg campaign, were especially useful for screening, reconnaissance, and advance guard actions in which they seized and held important hills, river crossings, and road junctions pending the arrival of infantry. During the morning hours of July 1, this was the role played by Union horsemen on the ridges north and west of Gettysburg.

By noon both the I and the XI Corps of the Army of the Potomac had joined in the battle, and Lt. Gen. Richard S. Ewell's Corps of Confederates had moved to support Hill. The latter, advancing from the north, broke the lines of the XI Corps and drove the Federals back through Gettysburg. The Union infantry rallied behind artillery positioned on Cemetery and Culp's Hills south of the town. Lee, who reached the field about 2 P.M. ordered Ewell to take Cemetery Hill, "if possible." But Ewell failed to press his advantage, and the Confederates settled into positions extending in a great curve from northeast of Culp's Hill, westward through Gettysburg, thence south on Seminary Ridge. During the night the Federals, enjoying interior lines, moved troops onto the key points of Culp's Hill, Cemetery Hill, Cemetery Ridge, and Little Round Top.

Meade had completed his dispositions by the morning of July 2, and his line was strong except in two places. In the confusion, Little Round Top was occupied only by a signal station when the supporting cavalry was dispatched to guard the army trains and not replaced; and the commander of the III Corps, Maj. Gen. Daniel E. Sickles, on his own responsibility moved his line forward from the south end of Cemetery Ridge to higher ground near the Peach Orchard, so that his corps lay in an exposed salient. By early afternoon, seven corps were arrayed along the Union battle line.

On the Confederate side, Lee had not been able to attack early; reconnaissance took time, and Longstreet's leading division did not arrive until afternoon. Generals in the Civil War tried to combine frontal assaults with envelopments and flanking movements, but the difficulty of timing and co-ordinating the movements of such large bodies of men in broken terrain made intricate maneuvers difficult. The action on the second day at Gettysburg graphically illustrates the problem. Lee wanted Longstreet to outflank the Federal left, part of Hill's corps was to strike the center, while Ewell's corps was to envelop the right flank of Meade's army. The attack did not start until 3 P.M. when Longstreet's men, having deployed on unfamiliar ground under a corps commander who preferred to take a defensive stance, advanced toward Little Round Top. The brigade was the basic maneuver element, and it formed for the attack with regiments in a two-rank line. Divisions usually attacked in columns of brigades, the second 150 to 300 yards behind the first, the third a similar distance behind the second. Skirmishers protected the flanks if no units were posted on either side. But such textbook models usually degenerated under actual fighting conditions, and so it was with Longstreet's attack. Divisions and brigades went in piecemeal, but with savage enthusiasm. Attacks started in close order as most men were using single-shot muzzle-loaders and had to stand shoulder to shoulder in order to get enough firepower and shock effect. But intervals between units soon increased under fire, troops often scattered for cover and concealment behind stone walls and trees, and thereafter units advanced by short rushes supported by fire from neighboring units. Thus, by late afternoon the smoke of battle was thick over the fields south of Gettysburg and the cries of the wounded mingled with the crash of musketry. The whole sector had become a chaos of tangled battle lines.

At this point Meade's chief engineer, Brig. Gen. Gouverneur Warren, discovering that no infantry held Little Round Top, persuaded the commander of the V Corps, Maj. Gen. George Sykes, to send two brigades and some artillery to the hill. They arrived just in time to hold the summit against a furious Confederate assault. When this attack bogged down, Longstreet threw a second division against Sickles' troops in the Peach Orchard and Wheatfield; this cracked the Federal line and drove as far as Cemetery Ridge before Meade's reserves halted it. Lee then ordered his troops to attack progressively from right to left and one of Hill's divisions assaulted Cemetery Ridge in piecemeal fashion, but was driven off. On the north Ewell attacked about 6 P.M. and captured some abandoned trenches, but Federals posted behind stone walls proved too strong. As the day ended the Federals held all their main positions. The Confederates had fought hard and with great bravery, but the progressive attack, which ignored the principle of mass, never engaged the Union front decisively at any point. The assaults were delivered against stoutly defended, prepared positions; Malvern Hill and Fredericksburg had shown this tactic to be folly, although perhaps Lee's successes against prepared positions at Chancellorsville led him to overoptimism.

Meade, after requesting the opinions of his corps commanders, decided to defend , rather than attack, on July 3. He also estimated that Lee, having attacked his right and left, would try for his center. He was right. Lee had planned to launch a full-scale, co-ordinated attack all along the line but then changed his mind in favor of a massive frontal assault by 10 brigades from four divisions of Longstreet's and Hill's corps against the Union center, which was held by Maj. Gen. Winfield Scott Hancock's II Corps. The assault was to be preceded by a massive artillery barrage.

The infantry's main support during the war was provided by field artillery. Rifled guns of relatively long range were available, but the soldiers preferred the 6-pounder and 12-pounder smoothbores. Rifled cannon were harder to clean; their projectiles were not as effective; their greater range could not always be effectively used because development of a good indirect fire control system would have to await the invention of the field telephone and the radio; and, finally, the rifled guns had flat trajectories, whereas the higher trajectories of the smoothbores enabled gunners to put fire on reverse slopes. Both types of cannon were among the artillery of the two armies at Gettysburg.

At 1 P.M. on July 3 Confederate gunners opened fire from approximately 140 pieces along Seminary Ridge in the greatest artillery bombardment witnessed on the American continent up to that time. For two hours the barrages continued, but did little more than tear up ground, destroy a few caissons, and expend ammunition. The Union artillery in the sector, numbering only 80 guns, had not been knocked out. It did stop firing in order to conserve ammunition, and the silence seemed to be a signal that the Confederates should begin their attack.

Under command of Maj. Gen. George E. Pickett, 15,000 men emerged from the woods on Seminary Ridge, dressed their three lines as if on parade, and began the mile-long, 20-minute march toward Cemetery Ridge. The assault force—47 regiments altogether—moved at a walk until it neared the Union lines, then broke into a run. Union artillery, especially 40 Napoleons on the south end of the ridge and some rifled guns on Little Round Top, opened fire, enfiladed the gray ranks, and forced Pickett's right over to the north. Despite heavy casualties the Confederates kept their formation until they came within rifle and canister range of the II Corps, and by then the lines and units were intermingled. The four brigades composing the left of Pickett's first line were heavily hit but actually reached and crossed the stone wall defended by Brig. Gen. John Gibbon's 2d Division of the II Corps, only to be quickly cut down or captured. Pickett's survivors withdrew to Seminary Ridge, and the fighting was over except for a suicidal mounted charge by Union cavalry, which Longstreet's right flank units easily halted. Both sides had fought hard and with great valor, for among 90,000 effective Union troops and 75,000 Confederates there were more than 51,000 casualties. The Army of the Potomac lost 3,155 killed, 14,529 wounded, and 5,365 prisoners and missing. Of the Army of Northern Virginia, 3,903 were killed, 18,735 wounded, and 5,425 missing and prisoners. If Chancellorsville was Lee's finest battle, Gettysburg was clearly his worst; yet the reverse did not unnerve him or reduce his effectiveness as a commander. The invasion had patently failed, and he retired at once toward the Potomac. As that river was flooded, it was several days before he was able to cross. President Lincoln, pleased over Meade's defensive victory and elated over Grant's capture of Vicksburg, thought the war could end in 1863 if Meade launched a resolute pursuit and destroyed Lee's army on the north bank of the Potomac. But Meade's own army was too mangled, and the Union commander moved cautiously, permitting Lee to return safely to Virginia on July 13.

Gettysburg was the last important action in the eastern

theater in 1863. Lee and Meade maneuvered against each other in Virginia, but there was no more fighting. After Gettysburg and Vicksburg the center of strategic gravity shifted to Tennessee.

The Chickamauga Campaign

One week before the surrender of Vicksburg and the Union victory at Gettysburg, General Rosecrans moved out of Murfreesboro, Tennessee, and headed for Chattanooga, one of the most important cities in the south because of its location. *(See Map 12)* It was a main junction on the rail line linking Richmond with Knoxville and Memphis. President Lincoln had long recognized the importance of railroads in this area. In 1862 he said, "To take and hold the railroad at or east of Cleveland [near Chattanooga], in East Tennessee, I think fully as important as the taking and holding of Richmond." Furthermore, at Chattanooga the Tennessee River cuts through the parallel ridges of the Appalachian Mountains and forms a natural gateway to either north or south. By holding the city, the Confederates could threaten Kentucky and prevent a Union penetration of the southeastern part of the Confederacy. If the Union armies pushed through Chattanooga, they would be in position to attack Atlanta, Savannah, or even the Carolinas and Richmond from the rear. As Lincoln told Rosecrans in 1863, "If we can hold Chattanooga and East Tennessee I think the rebellion must dwindle and die."

After the spring and summer campaigns in the east, the Davis government in Richmond approved a movement by Longstreet's corps of Lee's army to the west to reinforce the hard-pressed Bragg. Longstreet's move—a 900-mile trip by rail—involving some 10,000–15,000 men and six batteries of artillery, began on September 9. But a force under Burnside, now commanding the Department of the Ohio, which was not part of Rosecrans' command, had penetrated the Cumberland Gap and driven the Confederates from Knoxville; Longstreet had to go around by way of Savannah and Augusta to Atlanta, Georgia. and did not reach Bragg until September 18. The rail

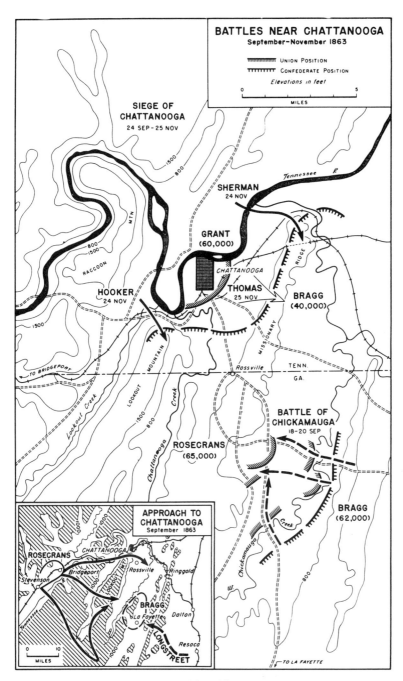

BATTLES NEAR CHATTANOOGA
September–November 1863

UNION POSITION
CONFEDERATE POSITION
Elevations in feet

0   5
MILES

SIEGE OF
CHATTANOOGA
24 SEP–25 NOV

Tennessee R.

SHERMAN
24 NOV

GRANT
(60,000)

1500
800

RACCOON
MTN

CHATTANOOGA

RIDGE

HOOKER
24 NOV

THOMAS
25 NOV

BRAGG
(40,000)

MISSIONARY

1500

TO BRIDGEPORT

LOOKOUT MOUNTAIN

Rossville

TENN.
GA.

Lookout Creek

LOOKOUT CREEK

Chattanooga Creek

1500
800

BATTLE OF
CHICKAMAUGA
18–20 SEP

ROSECRANS
(65,000)

BRAGG
(62,000)

Chickamauga Creek

800

TO LA FAYETTE

**APPROACH TO
CHATTANOOGA**
September 1863

ROSECRANS

CHATTANOOGA

Rossville

Ringgold

Bridgeport

LOOKOUT MT

Stevenson

BRAGG
La Fayette

Dalton

LONGSTREET

Resaca

0   10
MILES

Map 12

network was rickety, and Longstreet's soldiers quipped that such poor rolling stock had never been intended to carry such good soldiers. Movement of Longstreet's troops from Virginia was nevertheless an outstanding logistical achievement for the Confederates.

Rosecrans had meanwhile reached the north bank of the Tennessee River near Stevenson, Alabama, on August 20. By September 4 his forces were across and on their way toward Chattanooga. After months of delay Rosecrans had accomplished the feat of completely outmaneuvering Bragg without a major battle. He planned to get in behind Bragg from the southwest and bottle him up in Chattanooga, but the Confederate general saw through the scheme and slipped away southward, carefully planting rumors that his army was demoralized and in flight. Rosecrans then resolved to pursue, a decision that would have been wise if Bragg had been retreating in disorder.

There were few passes through the mountains and no good lateral roads. Rosecrans' army was dispersed in three columns over a 40-mile front in order to make use of the various passes. Bragg concentrated his army about September 10 at Lafayette, Georgia, some twenty miles south of Chattanooga. As his force was three times as large as any one of the Union columns, Bragg hopefully anticipated that he could defeat Rosecrans in detail. But his intelligence service failed him; he thought there were two, rather than three Union columns, and prepared plans accordingly. He first planned to strike what he thought was Rosecrans' right—actually the center—then the left, but his subordinates did not support him promptly, and the attacks were made in desultory fashion. Thus, twice in three days Bragg missed a fine opportunity to inflict a serious reverse upon the Federals because of his subordinates' failure to carry out orders.

By September 12 Rosecrans was at last aware that Bragg was not retreating in disorder but was preparing to fight. The Union commander ordered an immediate concentration, but this would take several days and in the meantime his corps were vulnerable. Although Bragg was usually speedy in executing attacks, this time he delayed, awaiting the arrival of Longstreet's corps. He intended to push Rosecrans southward away from Chattanooga into a mountain cul-de-sac where the Federals could be destroyed.

By September 17 Bragg was poised just east of Chickamauga Creek. *(Map 12)* (Chickamauga, translated from Cherokee into English, means "River of Death.") When Longstreet's three leading brigades arrived on September 18, Bragg decided to cross the Chickamauga and attack. But the Federals, with two corps almost concentrated, defended the fords so stoutly that only a few units got over that day. During the night more Confederates slipped across, and by morning of the 19th about three-fourths of Bragg's men were over.

Rosecrans' third corps went into the line on the 19th, and now Bragg faced a much stronger force than he had expected. The heavily wooded battlefield had few landmarks, and some units had difficulty maintaining direction. Fighting continued throughout much of the day, but by nightfall the Federals still controlled the roads to Chattanooga. That night Lee's "War-horse," Longstreet, arrived in person with two more brigades. He went looking for Bragg to report to him and lost his way in the woods. Encountering some soldiers, he asked them to identify their unit. When they replied with numbers—Confederate divisions were named for their commanders—he realized he was within Union lines, hastily rode off in the darkness, and eventually found Bragg. During the night Rosecrans regrouped and dug in.

Bragg decided to renew the attack the next day and to attack progressively from his right to left (sometimes known in military parlance as "oblique order"). He reorganized the Army of Tennessee into two wings under Polk and Longstreet with little regard for its existing corps organization. The attack began about 9 A.M. and hit Thomas' corps first. The Union line held until Rosecrans received an erroneous report that one of his units was not supported, and ordered another unit to move in and help. In the ensuing confusion, orders designated a unit which was already in line of battle. When this force obediently abandoned its position, Longstreet, just beginning his attack, saw the hole and drove into it at once. Thomas' right flank was bent back and most of the Union right wing simply melted from the field and streamed in rout back toward Chattanooga. Rosecrans, considering himself defeated, retired to Chattanooga to organize it for defense. Thomas, with about two-thirds of the disorganized army, stood fast and checked vicious attacks by

Longstreet and Polk until nightfall. This resolute stand and the valorous performance of the U.S. 19th Infantry won for Thomas and that unit the title "Rock of Chickamauga." A Confederate remembered that afternoon how "the dead were piled upon each other in ricks, like cord wood, to make passage for advancing columns. The sluggish Chickamauga ran red with human blood."

Bragg concluded that no decisive results could be attained that day. Polk, Longstreet, and Forrest pleaded with him to push the routed Federals and recapture Chattanooga. But 18,000 casualties (the Federals had lost only 1,500 less) so unnerved Bragg that he permitted Thomas to withdraw unmolested from the field to a blocking position extending from Missionary Ridge west to Lookout Mountain. Next day Thomas retired into Chattanooga. Polk wrote to President Davis of Bragg's "criminal negligence," and Forrest a week later insubordinately told the army commander, "You have played the part of a damned scoundrel, and are a coward and if you were any part of a man I would slap your jaws." Yet nothing could erase completely the fact that the Confederates had won a great victory and had Rosecrans' army bottled up in a trap.

Grant at Chattanooga

Rosecrans' army, having started out offensively, was now shut up in Chattanooga, as Bragg took up positions on Lookout Mountain and Missionary Ridge. The Union commander accepted investment and thus surrendered his freedom of action. Burnside, at Knoxville, was too far away to render immediate aid. There were no strong Confederate units north of Chattanooga, but Rosecrans' line of communications was cut away. The Nashville and Chattanooga Railroad, instead of running directly into the city, reached the river at Stevenson, crossed at Bridgeport southwest of Chattanooga, and ran through Confederate territory into town. River steamers could get to within only eight miles of Chattanooga; beyond, the Tennessee River was swift and narrow. Supplies therefore came over the mountains in wagons, but starting September 30 Confederate cavalry under Maj. Gen. Joseph Wheeler, one of Bragg's cavalry corps commanders, raided as far north as Murfreesboro. Though heavily and effectively opposed in his effort to tear up the railroad, he managed to destroy many precious Union supply wagons. With the mountain roads breaking down under the heavy traffic in wet weather, rations within Chattanooga ran short. Men went hungry, and horses, and mules began to die of starvation. Rosecrans prepared to reopen his line of communications by means of an overland route to the west. But this route was dominated by Confederate troops on Raccoon and Lookout Mountains. Additional troops to clear these strongpoints were required if the Army of the Cumberland was to survive.

Washington finally awoke to the fact than an entire Union army was trapped in Chattanooga and in danger of capture. In a midnight council meeting on September 23, the President met with Secretary Stanton, General Halleck, and others to determine what could be done. As General Meade was not then active in the east, they decided to detach two corps, or about 20,000 men, from the Army of the Potomac and send them by rail to Tennessee under the command of General Hooker, who had been without active command since his relief in June. The forces selected included 10 artillery batteries with over 3,000 mules and horses. The 1,157-mile journey involved four changes of trains, owing to differing gauges and lack of track connections, and eclipsed all other such troop movements by rail up to that time. The troops began to entrain at Manassas Junction and Bealton Station, Virginia, on September 25 and five days later the first trains arrived at Bridgeport, Alabama. Not all of the troops made such good time—for the majority of the infantry the trip consumed about nine days. And movement of the artillery, horses, mules, and baggage was somewhat slower. Combined with a waterborne movement of 17,000 men under Sherman from Mississippi, the reinforcement of the besieged Rosecrans was a triumph of skill and planning.

Chickamauga had caused Stanton and his associates to lose confidence in Rosecrans. For some time Lincoln had been dubious about Rosecrans, who, he said, acted "like a duck hit on the head" after Chickamauga, but he did not immediately choose a successor. Finally, about mid-October, he decided to unify command in the west and to vest it in General Grant, who still commanded the Army of the Tennessee. In October Stanton met Grant in Louisville and gave him orders which allowed him some discretion in selecting subordinates. Grant was appointed commander of the Military Division of the Mississippi, which embraced the Departments and Armies of the Ohio, the Cumberland, and the Tennessee, and included the vast area from the Alleghenies to the Mississippi River north of Banks' Department of the Gulf. Thomas replaced Rosecrans, and Sherman was appointed to command Grant's old army.

Now that Hooker had arrived, the line of communications, or the "cracker line" to the troops, could be reopened. Rosecrans had actually shaped the plan, and all that was needed was combat troops to execute it. On October 26 Hooker crossed the Tennessee at Bridgeport and attacked eastward. Within two days he had taken the spurs of the mountains, other Union troops had captured two important river crossings, and the supply line was open once more. Men, equipment, and food moved via riverboat and wagon road, bypassing Confederate strongpoints, to reinforce the besieged Army of the Cumberland.

In early November Bragg weakened his besieging army by sending Longstreet's force against Burnside at Knoxville. This move reduced Confederate strength to about 40,000 at about the same time that Sherman arrived with two army corps from Memphis. The troops immediately at hand under Grant— Thomas' Army of the Cumberland, two corps of Sherman's Army of the Tennessee, and two corps under Hooker from the Army of the Potomac—now numbered about 60,000. Grant characteristically decided to resume the offensive with his entire force.

The Confederates had held their dominant position for so long that they seemed to look on all of the Federals in Chattanooga as their ultimate prisoners. One day Grant went out to inspect the Union lines and he reached a point where Union and Confederate picket posts were not far apart. Not only did his own troops turn out the guard, but a smart set of Confederates came swarming out, formed a neat military rank, snapped to attention, and presented arms. Grant returned the salute and rode away. But plans were already afoot to divest the Confederates of some of their cockiness.

Grant planned to hit the ends of the Confederates' line at once. Hooker would strike at Lookout Mountain, and Sherman moving his army upstream across the river from Chattanooga, and crossing over by pontons, would hit the upper end of Missionary Ridge. While they were breaking the Confederate flanks, Thomas' men could make limited attacks on the center, and the Army of the Cumberland's soldiers, already nursing a bruised ego for the rout at Chickamauga, realized that in the eyes of the commanding general they were second-class troops.

Hooker took Lookout Mountain on November 24. On the same day Sherman crossed the Tennessee at the mouth of Chickamauga Creek and gained positions on the north end of Missionary Ridge. The next day his attacks bogged down as he attempted to drive southward along the Ridge. To help Sherman, Grant directed the Army of the Cumberland to take the rifle pits at the foot of the west slope of Missionary Ridge. These rifle pits were the first of three lines of Confederate trenches. Thomas' troops rushed forward, seized the pits, and then, having a score to settle with the Confederates positioned above them, took control of this phase of the battle. Coming under fire from the pits above and in front of them, the Federals simply kept on going. When Grant observed that movement he muttered that someone was going to sweat for it if the charge ended in disaster. But Thomas' troops drove all the way to the top, and in the afternoon Hooker swept the southern end of the ridge. The Federals then had the unusual experience of seeing a Confederate army disintegrate into precipitate retreat and beckoned to their Northern comrades: "My God! Come and see them run!" Grant pursued Bragg the next day, but one Confederate division skillfully halted the pursuit while Bragg retired into Georgia to regroup.

The battles around Chattanooga ended in one of the most complete Union victories of the war. Bragg's army was defeated, men and matériel captured, and the Confederates driven south. The mountainous defense line which the Confederates had hoped to hold had been pierced; the rail center of Chattanooga

93

was permanently in Union hands; and the rich, food-producing eastern Tennessee section was lost to the Confederacy. Relief had come at last for the Union sympathizers in eastern Tennessee. With Chattanooga secured as a base, the way was open for an invasion of the lower South.

CHAPTER 4

1864

From Bull Run to Chattanooga, the Union armies had fought their battles without benefit of either a grand strategy or a supreme field commander. During the final year of the war the people of the North grew restless, and as the election of 1864 approached, many of them advocated a policy of making peace with the Confederacy. President Lincoln never wavered. Committed to the policy of destroying the armed power of the Confederacy, he sought a general who could pull all the threads of an emerging strategy together, and then concentrate the Union armies and their supporting naval power against the secessionists. After Vicksburg in July 1863, Lincoln leaned more and more toward Grant as the man whose strategic thinking and resolution would lead the Union armies to final victory.

It is the strategic moves of the armies during the last year of the war, rather than the tactical details, that are most instructive.

Strategy of Annihilation and Unity of Command

Acting largely as his own General in Chief after McClellan's removal in early 1862, Mr. Lincoln had watched the Confederates fight from one ephemeral victory to another inside their cockpit of northern Virginia. In the western theater, Union armies, often operating independently of one another, had scored great victories at key terrain points. But their hold on the communications base at Nashville was always in jeopardy as long as the elusive armies of the Confederacy could escape to

95

fight another day at another key point. The twin, unco-ordinated victories at Gettysburg and Vicksburg, 900 miles apart, only pointed up the North's need for an over-all strategic plan and a general who could carry it out.

Having cleared the Mississippi River, Grant wrote to Halleck and the President about the opportunities now open to his army. Grant first called for the consolidation of the autonomous western departments and the co-ordination of their individual armies. After this great step, he proposed to isolate the area west of the line Chattanooga–Atlanta–Montgomery–Mobile. Within this region, Grant urged a "massive rear attack" that would take Union armies in the Gulf Department under Maj. Gen. Nathaniel P. Banks and Grant's Army of the Tennessee to Mobile and up the Alabama River to Montgomery. The U.S. Navy would play a major role in this attack. Simultaneously, Rosecrans was to advance overland through Chattanooga to Atlanta. All military resources within this isolated area would be destroyed.

Lincoln vetoed Grant's plan in part by deferring the Mobile–Montgomery phase. The President favored a demonstration by Banks up the Red River to Shreveport in order to show the American flag to Napoleon III's interlopers in Mexico, and Banks' Department of the Gulf was left out of the consolidation of the other western commands under Grant in October 1863.

After his own victory at Chattanooga in November, Grant wasted few hours in writing the President what he thought the next strategic moves should be. As a possible winter attack, Grant revived the touchy Mobile campaign while the Chat-tanooga victors were gathering strength for a spring offensive to Atlanta. Grant reasoned that Lee would vacate Virginia and shift strength toward Atlanta. For the Mobile–Montgomery plan, Grant asked for Banks' resources in the Gulf Department. Lincoln again balked because the Texas seacoast would be abandoned. Grant's rebuttal explained that Napoleon III would really be impressed with a large Army-Navy operation against Mobile Bay. The Red River campaign, Grant believed, would not deter Napoleon III. The President told Grant again that he had to heed the demands of Union diplomacy, but at the same time he encouraged Grant to enlarge his strategic proposals to include estimates for a grand Federal offensive for the coming spring of 1864.

Grant's plan of January 1864 projected a four-pronged continental attack. In concert, the four armies were to move on Atlanta, on Mobile—after Banks took Shreveport—on Lee's communications by a campaign across the middle of North Carolina on the axis New Bern–Neuse River–Goldsboro–Raleigh–Greensboro, and on Lee's Army of Northern Virginia in the hope of defeating it in an open battle. Lincoln opposed the North Carolina phase, fearing that Grant's diversion of 60,000 effective bayonets from formations covering Washington was too dangerous. Lincoln knew that Lee's eyes were always fixed on the vast amount of supplies in the depots around the Washington area.

Though Lincoln scuttled some of Grant's professional schemes, he never lost his esteem for Grant's enthusiasm and intelligence. In February 1864 Congress revived Scott's old rank of lieutenant general, to which Grant was promoted on March 9. Lincoln relieved Halleck as General in Chief, ordered Grant to Washington to assume Halleck's post, and during March the President, the new General in Chief, and the Secretary of War ironed out top-level command arrangements which had plagued every President since the War of 1812. Lincoln and Stanton relinquished powerful command, staff, and communications tools to Grant. Stanton, greatly impressed with Grant's public acclaim, cautioned his General Staff Bureau chiefs to heed Grant's needs and timetables.

In twentieth century terms, Grant was a theater commander. As General in Chief, he reported directly to the President and Secretary of War, keeping them informed about the broad aspects of his strategic plans and telling them in advance of his armies' needs. Grant removed himself from the politics of Washington and established his headquarters in northern Virginia. Though he planned to go quickly to troubled spots, Grant elected to accompany Meade's Army of the Potomac in order to assess Lee's moves and their effects on the other columns of the Union Army. By rail or steamboat, Grant was never far from

Lincoln, and in turn the President visited Grant frequently. To tie his far-flung commands together, Grant employed a vast telegraph system.

In a continental theater of war larger than Napoleon's at its zenith, Grant's job, administratively, eventually embraced four military divisions, totaling seventeen subcommands, wherein 500,000 combat soldiers would be employed. At Washington, Halleck operated a war room for Grant and eased his heavy burden of studying the several Army commanders' detailed field directives by preparing brief digests, thus saving the General in Chief many hours of reading detailed reports. Bearing the then nebulous title of "Chief of Staff, U.S. Army," Halleck had a major job in keeping Grant informed about supply levels at base depots and advance dumps in Nashville, St. Louis, City Point, Washington, Philadelphia, Louisville, and New York City. Under Stanton Quartermaster General Montgomery C. Meigs, the most informed logistician and supply manager of his day, dispatched men and munitions to Grant's subcommands according to a strategic timetable. As the spring offensive progressed, Stanton, Halleck, and Meigs gave Grant a rear-area team that grasped the delicate balance between theater objectives and the logistical support required to achieve them.

Grant spent the month of April on the Rapidan front developing his final strategic plan for ending the war. In essence, he recapped all of his views on the advantages to be gained from his victories in the western theater. He added some thoughts about moving several Federal armies, aided by naval power when necessary, toward a common center in a vast, concentrated effort. He planned to stop the Confederates from using their interior lines. He intended to maneuver Lee away from the Rapidan Wilderness and defeat the Army of Northern Virginia in open terrain by a decisive battle. Another Union force collected from the Atlantic seaport towns of the deep South was to cut the James–Appomattox River line to sever Lee's rail and road links with the other parts of the Confederacy. Simultaneously, Sherman's group of armies would execute a wide wheeling movement through the South to complete the envelopment of the whole country east of the Mississippi. Banks was still scheduled to make the attack through Mobile. As Lincoln described the plan, "Those not skinning can hold a leg."

By mid-April 1864 Grant had issued specific orders to each commander of the four Federal armies that were to execute the grand strategy. In round numbers the Union armies were sending 300,000 combat troops against 150,000 Confederates defending the invasion paths. Meade's Army of the Potomac and Burnside's independent IX Corps, a combined force of 120,000 men, constituted the major attack column under Grant's over-all direction. The enemy had 63,000 troops facing Grant along the Rapidan. Two subsidiary thrusts were to support Meade's efforts. Commanding a force of 33,000 men, Butler with his Army of the James was to skirt the south bank of the James, menace Richmond, take it if possible, and destroy the railroads below Petersburg. Acting as a right guard in the Shenandoah Valley, Maj. Gen. Franz Sigel's 23,000 Federals were to advance on Lee's rail hub at Lynchburg, Virginia. With the northern Virginia triangle under attack, in the continental center of the line Sherman's 100,000 men were to march on Atlanta, annihilating Joseph E. Johnston's 65,000 soldiers, and devastating the resources of central Georgia. On the continental right of the line, Banks was to disengage as soon as possible along the Red River and with Rear Adm. David C. Farragut's blockading squadron in the Gulf of Mexico make a limited amphibious landing against Mobile. The day for advance would be announced early in May.

In rising from regimental command to General in Chief, Grant had learned much from experience, and if he sometimes made mistakes he rarely repeated them. Not a profound student of the literature of warfare, he had become, by the eve of his grand campaign, one of those rare leaders who combine the talents of the strategist, tactician, and logistician and who marry those talents to the principle of the offensive. His operations, especially the "rear mass attack," were models of the execution of the principles of war. He was calm in crisis; reversals and disappointments did not unhinge his cool judgment. He mastered the dry-as-dust details of a logistical system and used common sense in deciding when to use the horse-drawn wagon, the railroad, or the steamboat in his strategic moves. Above all, Grant understood and applied the principle of modern war that the destruction of the enemy's economic resources is as necessary as the annihilation of the enemy's armies.

Lee Cornered at Richmond

On the morning of May 4, 1864, Meade and Sherman moved out to execute Grant's grand strategy. The combat strength of the Army of the Potomac, slimmed down from seven unwieldy corps, consisted of three infantry corps of 25,000 rifles each and a cavalry corps. Commanding the 12,000-man cavalry corps was Maj. Gen. Philip H. Sheridan, an energetic leader brought east by Grant on Halleck's recommendation. Meade again dispersed his cavalry, using troopers as messengers, pickets, and train guards, but young Sheridan, after considerable argument, eventually succeeded in concentrating all of his sabers as a separate combat arm. Grant reorganized Burnside's IX Corps of 20,000 infantrymen, held it as a strategic reserve for a time, and then assigned the IX Corps to Meade's army. Lee's army, now 70,000 strong, was also organized into a cavalry and three infantry corps.

Grant and Lee were at the height of their careers and this was their first contest of wills. Having the initiative, Grant crossed the Rapidan and decided to go by Lee's right, rather than his left. *(Map 13)* First, Grant wanted to rid himself of the need to use an insecure railroad with limited capacity back to Alexandria, Virginia. Second, he wanted to end the Army of the Potomac's dependence on a train of 4,000 wagons; the Army's mobility was hobbled by having to care for 60,000 animals. Finally, Grant wanted to use the advantages of Virginia's tidewater rivers and base his depots on the Chesapeake Bay. He was willing to accept the risk inherent in moving obliquely across Lee's front in northern Virginia.

With little room for maneuver, Grant was forced to advance through the Wilderness, where Hooker had come to grief the year before. As the army column halted near Chancellorsville to allow the wagon trains to pass the Rapidan, on May 5 Lee

100

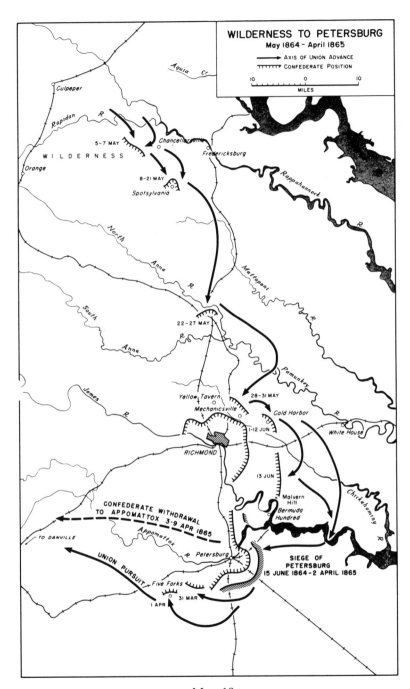

WILDERNESS TO PETERSBURG
May 1864 – April 1865

→ AXIS OF UNION ADVANCE
ⱅⱅⱅⱅⱅ CONFEDERATE POSITION

10   0   10
MILES

Aquia Cr

Culpeper

Rapidan R

5-7 MAY   Chancellorsville
WILDERNESS   Fredericksburg

Orange

8-21 MAY
Spotsylvania

Rappahannock R

North Anna R

Mattaponi

South Anna R

22-27 MAY

R

Pamunkey R

James R   Yellow Tavern   28-31 MAY
                       Mechanicsville   Cold Harbor
                                              White House
                       RICHMOND   1-12 JUN

                                       13 JUN
                                              Malvern
CONFEDERATE WITHDRAWAL   Hill
TO APPOMATTOX 3-9 APR 1865   Bermuda
                                              Hundred   Chickahominy R
TO DANVILLE   Appomattox R

UNION PURSUIT   Petersburg   SIEGE OF
              Five Forks   PETERSBURG
                        31 MAR   15 JUNE 1864-2 APRIL 1865
              1 APR

Map 13

struck at Meade's right flank. Grant and Meade swung their corps into line and hit hard. The fighting in the battle of the Wilderness consisting of assault, defense, and counterattack, was close and desperate in tangled woods and thickets. Artillery could not be brought to bear. The dry woods caught fire and some of the wounded died miserably in the flame and smoke. On May 6 Lee attacked again. Longstreet's I Corps, arriving late in battle but as always in perfect march order, drove the Federals back. Longstreet himself received a severe neck wound, inflicted in error by his own men, that took him out of action until October 1864. Lee, at a decisive moment in the battle, his fighting blood aroused to a white heat, attempted to lead an assault in person; but men of the Texas brigade with whom Lee was riding persuaded the southern leader to go to the rear and direct the battle as their Army commander. On May 7 neither side renewed the battle.

Now came the critical test of Grant's execution of strategy. He had been worsted, though not really beaten, by Lee, a greater antagonist than Bragg, Joseph E. Johnston, and Pemberton. After an encounter with Lee, each of the former Army of the Potomac commanders, McClellan, Burnside, and Hooker, had retired north of the Rappahannock River and postponed any further clashes with that great tactician. But Grant was of a different breed. He calmly ordered his lead corps to move south toward Spotsylvania as rapidly as possible to get around Lee's flank and interpose the Army of the Potomac between Lee and Richmond.

Lee detected Grant's march and, using roads generally parallel to Grant's, also raced toward the key road junction at Spotsylvania. J. E. B. Stuart's cavalry harassed and slowed Grant; Lee arrived first and quickly built strong earth-and-log trenches over commanding ground which covered the roads leading to Richmond. In this crossroads race, Sheridan's cavalry would have been useful, but Meade had dissipated the cavalry corps' strength by deploying two divisions of horse to guard his already well-protected trains. Sheridan and Meade argued once again over the use of cavalry, and the General in Chief backed Sheridan, allowing him now to concentrate his cavalry arm. Grant gave Sheridan a free hand in order to stop Stuart's raids. Leading his corps southward in a long ride toward Richmond, its objective a decisive charge against Stuart, Sheridan did the job. He fought a running series of engagements that culminated in a victory at Yellow Tavern, in which the gallant Stuart was mortally wounded. The South was already short of horses and mules, and Sheridan's 16-day raid ended forever the offensive power of Lee's mounted arm.

For four days beginning May 9 Meade struck repeatedly at Lee's roadblock at Spotsylvania but was beaten back. Twice the Federals broke through the trenches and divided Lee's army, but in each case the attackers became disorganized. Supporting infantry did not or could not close in, and Confederate counterattacks were delivered with such ferocity that the breakthroughs could be neither exploited nor held. On the morning of the 11th, Grant wrote Halleck: "I propose to fight it out on this line if it takes all summer." On May 20, having decided the entrenchments were too strong to capture, Grant sideslipped south again, still trying to envelop Lee's right flank.

With smaller numbers, Lee skillfully avoided Grant's trap and refused to leave entrenched positions and be destroyed in open battle. Lee retired to the North Anna River and dug in. Grant then continued to move south, to his left, in a daring and difficult tactical maneuver. Butler had meanwhile advanced up the peninsula toward Richmond, but Beauregard outmaneuvered him in May and bottled up Butler's men at Bermuda Hundred between the James and Appomattox Rivers. Eventually Butler and Banks, who did not take Mobile, were removed from command for their failure to carry out their assignments in the grand strategy.

Lee easily made his way into the Richmond defenses with his right flank on the Chickahominy and his center at Cold Harbor, the site of the Gaines' Mill action in 1862. The front extended for eight miles. On June 3 Grant assaulted Lee's center at Cold Harbor. Though bravely executed, the attack was badly planned. The Confederates repulsed it with gory efficiency, and Grant later regretted that he had ever made the attempt. Cold Harbor climaxed a month of heavy fighting in which Grant's forces had casualties totaling about 55,000 as against about 32,000 for those of Lee. After Cold Harbor, Grant executed a brilliant maneuver in the face of the enemy. All Union corps were on the north bank of the deep, wide James by June 14 and crossed over a 2,100-foot ponton bridge, the longest up to that time in modern history. Having established a new and modern base depot at City Point, complete with a railroad line to the front, Grant on June 18, 1864, undertook siege operations at Petersburg below Richmond, an effort which continued into the next year.

After forty-four days of continuous fighting, Lee was fixed finally in position warfare, a war of trenches and sieges, conducted ironically enough by two masters of mobile warfare. Mortars were used extensively, and heavy siege guns were brought up on railway cars. Grant still sought to get around Lee's right and hold against Lee's left to prevent him from shortening his line and achieving a higher degree of concentration. When Lee moved his lines to counter Grant, the two commanders were, in effect, maneuvering their fortifications.

Now that Lee was firmly entrenched in front of Grant, and could spare some men, he decided to ease the pressure with one of his perennial raids up the Shenandoah Valley toward Washington. Confederate Maj. Gen. Jubal A. Early's corps in early July advanced against Maj. Gen. David Hunter, who had replaced Sigel. Hunter, upon receiving confused orders from Halleck, retired up the valley. When he reached the Potomac, he turned west into the safety of the Appalachians and uncovered Washington. Early saw his chance and drove through Maryland. Delayed by a Union force on July 9 near Frederick, he reached the northern outskirts of Washington on July 11 and skirmished briskly in the vicinity of Fort Stevens. Abraham Lincoln and Quartermaster General Meigs were interested spectators. At City Point, Grant had received the news of Early's raid calmly. Using his interior waterway, he embarked the men of his VI Corps for the capital, where they landed on the 11th. When Early realized he was engaging troops from the Army of the Potomac, he managed to escape the next day.

Grant decided that Early had eluded the Union's superior forces because they had not been under a single commander. He abolished four separate departments and formed them into one, embracing Washington, western Maryland, and the Shenandoah Valley. In August, Sheridan was put in command with orders to follow Early to the death. Sheridan spent the remainder of the year in the valley, employing and co-ordinating his infantry, cavalry, and artillery in a manner that has won the admiration of military students ever since. He met and defeated Early at Winchester and Fisher's Hill in September and shattered him at Cedar Creek in October. To stop further raids and prevent Lee from feeding his army on the crops of that fertile region, Sheridan devastated the Shenandoah Valley.

Sherman's Great Wheel to the East

On March 17, 1864, Grant had met with Sherman at Nashville and told him his role in the grand strategy. Sherman, like Grant, held two commands. As Division of the Mississippi commander, he was responsible for the operation and defense of a vast logistical system that reached from a communications zone at St. Louis, Louisville, and Cincinnati to center on a large base depot at Nashville. Strategically, Nashville on the Cumberland River rivaled Washington, D.C., in importance. A 90-mile military railroad, built and operated by Union troops, gave Nashville access to steamboats plying the Tennessee River. Connected with Louisville by rail, Nashville became one vast storehouse and corral. If the city was destroyed, the Federal forces would have to fall back to the Ohio River line. Wearing his other hat, Sherman was a field commander with three armies under his direction.

With the promise of the return of his two crack divisions from the Red River expedition by May 1864 and with a splendid administrative system working behind him, Sherman was ready to leave Chattanooga in the direction of Atlanta. *(Map 14)* His mission was to destroy Johnston's armies and capture Atlanta, which after Richmond was the most important industrial center in the Confederacy. With 254 guns, Sherman matched his three small armies, and a separate cavalry command—a total force of more than 100,000 men—against Joseph E. Johnston's Army of Tennessee and the Army of Mississippi including Wheeler's cavalry, consisting of 65,000 men.

Sherman moved out on May 4, 1864, the same day the Army of the Potomac crossed the Rapidan. Johnston, realizing how seriously he was outnumbered, decided to go on the defensive,

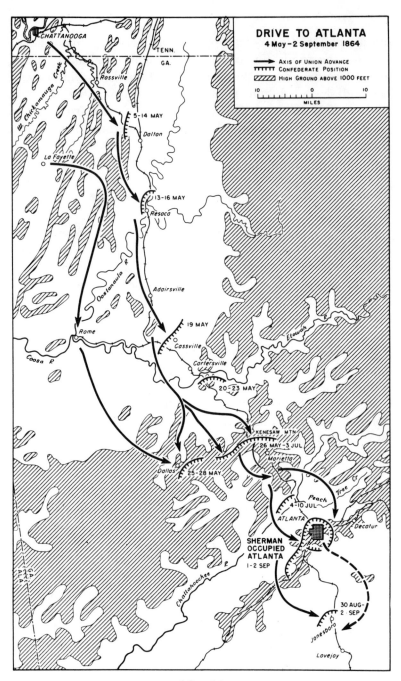

DRIVE TO ATLANTA
4 May–2 September 1864

→ AXIS OF UNION ADVANCE
⊥⊥⊥⊥⊥ CONFEDERATE POSITION
▨ HIGH GROUND ABOVE 1000 FEET

10   0   10
MILES

CHATTANOOGA

TENN.
GA.

Rossville

W. Chickamauga Creek

5–14 MAY
Dalton

La Fayette

13–16 MAY
Resaca

Oostanaula R.

Adairsville

19 MAY
Cassville

Etowah R.

Rome
Cartersville

Coosa R.
20–23 MAY

KENESAW MTN.
26 MAY–3 JUL
Marietta

Dallas
25–28 MAY

Peach Tree Cr.

4–10 JUL
ATLANTA
Decatur

SHERMAN
OCCUPIED
ATLANTA
1–2 SEP

GA.
ALA.

Chattahoochee R.

30 AUG–
2 SEP
Jonesboro

Lovejoy

Map 14

preserve his forces intact, hold Atlanta, and delay Sherman as long as possible. There was always the hope that the North would grow weary of the costly struggle and that some advocate of peaceful settlement might defeat Abraham Lincoln in the election of 1864. From May 4 through mid-July, the two forces maneuvered against each other. There were daily fights but few large-scale actions. As Sherman pushed south, Johnston would take up a strong position and force Sherman to halt, deploy, and reconnoiter. Sherman would then outflank Johnston, who in turn would retire to a new line and start the process all over again. On June 27 Sherman, unable to maneuver because the roads were muddy and seriously concerned by the unrest in his armies brought about by constant and apparently fruitless marching, decided to assault Johnston at Kennesaw Mountain. This attack against prepared positions, like the costly failure at Cold Harbor, was beaten back. Sherman returned to maneuver and forced Johnston back to positions in front of Atlanta.

Johnston had done his part well. He had accomplished his missions and had so slowed Sherman that Sherman covered only 100 miles in 74 days. Johnston, his forces intact, was holding strong positions in front of Atlanta, his main base; but by this time Jefferson Davis had grown impatient with Johnston and his tactics of cautious delay. In July he replaced him with Lt. Gen. John B. Hood, a much more impetuous commander.

On July 20, while Sherman was executing a wide turning movement around the northeast side of Atlanta, Hood left his fortifications and attacked at Peach Tree Creek. When Sherman beat him off, Hood pulled back into the city. While Sherman made ready to invest, Hood attacked again and failed again. Sherman then tried cavalry raids to cut the railroads, just as Johnston had during the advance from Chattanooga, but Sherman's raids had as little success as Johnston's. Sherman then began extending fortifications on August 31. Hood, who had dissipated his striking power in his assaults, gave up and retired to northwest Alabama, and Sherman marched into Atlanta on the first two days of September. Sherman hoped that Mobile had fallen, and a shorter line for his supplies by way of Montgomery, Alabama, or still better by the lower Chattahoochee to Columbus, Georgia, was open. Admiral Farragut had entered Mobile Bay on August 5, 1864, but had no troops to take Mobile itself.

The fall of Atlanta gave President Lincoln's campaign for re-election in 1864 a tremendous boost. In addition, the psychological lift given the Union by Admiral Farragut's personal heroism in the battle of Mobile Bay greatly added to Lincoln's prestige.

Atlanta was only a halfway point in Sherman's vast wheel from the western theater toward the rear of Lee's Army of Northern Virginia. Abandoning the idea of catching up with Hood, Sherman by telegraph outlined his next strategic move to Lincoln and Grant in early September 1864. Sherman's two proposals proved him an able strategist as well as a consummately bold and aggressive commander. To defend Nashville, he suggested that he send two corps, 30,000 men, back to Thomas, where that commander would raise and train more men and be in position to hold Tennessee if Hood came north. To carry the offensive against the economic heart of the Confederacy, Sherman recommended that he himself take four corps—62,000 men—cut his own communications, live off the country, and march to the seacoast through Georgia, devastating and laying waste all farms, railways, and storehouses in his path. Whether he arrived at Pensacola, Charleston, or Savannah, Sherman reasoned he could hold a port, make contact with the U.S. Navy, and be refitted by Stanton and Meigs. Meigs promised to do the logistical job, and Lincoln and Grant, though their reaction to the plan was less than enthusiastic, accepted it in a show of confidence in Sherman.

Before marching out of Atlanta, Sherman's engineers put selected buildings to the torch and destroyed all railroads in the vicinity. On November 12, moving away from the Nashville depots toward Savannah, the Division of the Mississippi troops broke telegraphic contact with Grant. They had twenty days' emergency rations in their wagons, but planned to replenish them by living off the country. Operating on a 60-mile-wide front, unimpeded by any Confederate force, Sherman's army systematically burned and destroyed what it did not need. The march became something of a rowdy excursion. Sherman's campaign, like Sheridan's in the Shenandoah, anticipated the economic warfare and strategic aerial bombardments of the twentieth century. Yet the victims of his methods could hardly

108

be blamed if they regarded Sherman's strategy as an excuse for simple thievery.

On December 10 Sherman, having broken the classic pattern by moving away from his logistical base, arrived in front of Savannah. Confederate forces evacuated the seaport on December 21 and Sherman offered it to the nation as a Christmas present. Awaiting him offshore was Meigs' floating seatrain, which enabled him to execute the last phase of Grant's strategy, a thrust north toward the line of the James River.

Thomas Protects the Nashville Base

Sherman, as the western theater commander, did not learn of Nashville's fate until he reached Savannah. He had planned Nashville's defense well enough by sending his IV and XXII Corps under Maj. Gen. John M. Schofield to screen Hood's northward move from Florence, Alabama. Schofield was to allow Thomas some time to assemble 50,000 men and strengthen Nashville. The aggressive Hood with his 30,000 men had lost a golden opportunity to trap Schofield at Spring Hill, Tennessee, on November 29, 1864. Unopposed, the Union troops made a night march across Hood's front to escape capture. Bitterly disappointed, Hood overtook Schofield the next day at Franklin.

Grant's continental timetable could have at this point been upset by Hood. Booty at Nashville might carry Hood to the Ohio or allow him to concentrate with Lee before Richmond. But Franklin turned into one of the Confederacy's most tragic battles. It commenced about 3:30 P.M. on November 30 and ended at dusk as Hood threw 18,000 of his veterans against a solidly entrenched force of Federals. Like Pickett's charge at Gettysburg, Hood's frontal assault gained nothing. He lost over 6,000 men, including 13 general officers. At nightfall Schofield brought his troops in behind Thomas' defenses at Nashville.

Hood was in a precarious position. He had been far weaker than Thomas to begin with; the battle of Franklin had further depleted his army; and, even worse, his men had lost confidence in their commander. The Federals in Nashville were securely emplaced in a city which they had been occupying for three years. Hood could do little more than encamp on high ground a few miles south of Nashville and wait. He could not storm the city; his force was too small to lay siege; to sidestep and go north was an open invitation to Thomas to attack his flank and rear; and to retreat meant disintegration of his army. He could only watch Thomas' moves.

Thomas, the Rock of Chickamauga, belonged to the last bootlace school of soldiering. In comparison with Grant and Sherman, he was slow; but he was also thorough. He had gathered and trained men and horses and was prepared to attack Hood on December 10, but an ice storm the day before made movement impossible. Grant and his superiors in Washington fretted at the delay, and the General in Chief actually started west to remove Thomas. But on December 15 Thomas struck like a sledgehammer in an attack that militarily students have regarded as virtually faultless.

Thomas' tactical plan was a masterly, co-ordinated attack. His heavily weighted main effort drove against Hood's left flank while a secondary attack aimed simultaneously at Hood's right. Thomas provided an adequate reserve and used cavalry to screen his flank and extend the envelopment of the enemy left. Hood, on the other hand, was overextended and his thin line was concave to the enemy, denying him the advantage of interior lines. Hood's reserve was inadequate, and his cavalry was absent on a minor mission.

The two-day battle proceeded according to Thomas' plan as the Federals fixed Hood's right while slashing savagely around the Confederate left flank. They broke Hood's first line on December 15, forcing the southerners to retire to a new line two miles to the rear. The Federals repeated their maneuver on the 16th, and by nightfall the three-sided battle had disintegrated into a rout of Hood's army. Broken and defeated, it streamed southward, protected from hotly pursuing Union cavalry only by the intrepid rear-guard action of Forrest's horsemen. The shattered Army of the Tennessee reached Tupelo, Mississippi, on January 10, 1865. It no longer existed as an effective fighting force; Hood was relieved of command and his scattered units were assigned to other areas of combat. The decisive battle of Nashville had eliminated one of the two great armies of the Confederacy from a shrinking chessboard.

CHAPTER 5

1865

Lee's Last 100 Days

President Lincoln was delighted with Savannah as a Christmas present, and in his congratulatory letter to Sherman and Grant the Commander in Chief said that he would leave the final phases of the war to his two leading professional soldiers. Accordingly, from City Point, Grant directed Sherman, on December 27, 1864, to march overland toward Richmond. At 3 P.M. on December 31, Sherman agreed to execute this last phase of Grant's continental sweep. In the final 100 days of the war, the two generals would clearly demonstrate the art of making principles of warfare come alive and prove that each principle was something more than a platitude. Each commander had a common objective: Grant and Meade would continue to hammer Lee; Sherman was to execute a devastating invasion northward through the Carolinas toward a juncture with Meade's Army of the Potomac, then on the line of the James River. Their strategy was simple. It called for the massing of strength and exemplified an economy of force. It would place Lee in an unmaneuverable position, cutting him off from all other Confederate commanders. Surprise would be achieved by reuniting all of Sherman's original corps when Schofield, moving from central Tennessee by rail, river, and ocean transport, arrived at the Carolina capes. Solidly based on a centralized logistical system with protected Atlantic seatrains at their side, Grant and Sherman were ready to end Lee's stay in Richmond.

Robert E. Lee, the master tactician, divining his end, wrote to Davis that the Confederates would have to concentrate their forces for a last-ditch stand. In February 1865 the Confederate Congress conferred supreme command of all Confederate armies on Lee, but it was an empty honor. Lee could no longer control events. Sherman moved through Columbia, South Carolina, in February, took Wilmington, North Carolina, the Confederacy's last port, then pushed on. Johnston, newly reappointed to a command, had the mission of stopping Sherman's forces, but could not. At Richmond and Petersburg toward the end of March, Grant renewed his efforts along a thirty-eight-mile front to get at Lee's right (west) flank. By now Sheridan's cavalry and the VI Corps had returned from the Shenandoah Valley, and the total force immediately under Grant numbered 101,000 infantry, 14,700 cavalry, and 9,000 artillery. Lee had 46,000 infantry, 6,000 cavalry, and 5,000 artillery.

On March 29 Grant began his move to the left. Sheridan and the cavalry pushed out ahead by way of Dinwiddie Court House in order to strike at Burke's Station, the intersection of the Southside and Danville Railroads, while Grant's main body moved to envelop Lee's right. But Lee, alerted to the threat, moved west. General A. P. Hill, who never stood on the defense if there was a chance to attack, took his corps out of its trenches and assaulted the Union left in the swampy forests around White Oak Road. He pushed General Warren's V Corps back at first, but Warren counterattacked and by March 31 had driven Hill back to his trenches. Next day Sheridan advanced to Five Forks, a road junction southwest of Petersburg, and there encountered a strong Confederate force under General Pickett— cavalry plus two infantry divisions—which Lee had dispatched to forestall Sheridan. Pickett attacked and drove Sheridan back to Dinwiddie Court House, but there Sheridan dug in and halted him. Pickett then entrenched at Five Forks instead of pulling back to make contact with Hill, whose failure to destroy Warren had left a gap between him and Pickett with Warren's corps in between. Sheridan, still formally the commander of the Army of the Shenandoah, had authority from Grant to take control of the nearby infantry corps of the Army of the Potomac. He wanted Warren to fall upon Pickett's exposed rear and destroy him, but Warren moved too slowly and Pickett consolidated his position. Next day Sheridan attacked again but failed

112

to destroy Pickett because Warren had moved his corps too slowly and put most of it in the wrong place. Sheridan, another devotee of the offensive principle who would not tolerate failure to engage the enemy, summarily relieved Warren of command.

Grant renewed his attack against Lee's right on April 2. The assault broke the Confederate line and forced it back northward. The Federals took the line of the Southside Railroad, and the Confederates withdrew toward Petersburg. Lee then pulled Longstreet's corps away from the shambles of Richmond to hold the line, and in this day's action Hill was killed. With his forces stretched thin, Lee had to abandon Richmond and the Petersburg fortifications. He struck out and raced west toward the Danville Railroad, hoping to get to Lynchburg or Danville, break loose, and eventually join forces with Johnston. But Grant had him in the open at last. He pursued relentlessly and speedily, with troops behind (east of) Lee and south of him on his left flank, while Sheridan dashed ahead with the cavalry to head Lee off. A running fight ensued from April 2 through 6. Ewell's corps was surrounded and captured at Sayler's Creek. Lee's rations ran out; his men began deserting and straggling. Finally, Sheridan galloped his men to Appomattox Court House, squarely athwart Lee's line of retreat.

Lee resolved that he could accomplish nothing more by fighting. He met Grant at the McLean House in Appomattox on April 9, 1865. The handsome, well-tailored Lee, the very epitome of southern chivalry, asked Grant for terms. Reserving all political questions for his own decision, Lincoln had authorized Grant to treat only on purely military matters. Grant, though less impressive in his bearing than Lee, was equally chivalrous. He accepted Lee's surrender, allowed 28,356 paroled Confederates to keep their horses and mules, furnished rations to the Army of Northern Virginia, and forbade the soldiers of the Army of the Potomac to cheer or fire salutes in celebration of victory over their old antagonists. Johnston surrendered to Sherman on April 26, twelve days after the assassination of the President. The last major trans-Mississippi force gave up the struggle on May 26, and the grim fighting was over.

Attrition in manpower had forced both South and North to turn from volunteers to conscription in order to keep their armies up to effective strength. The Confederate government had enacted a draft law as early as April 1862. Late in that year Union governors were no longer able to raise enough troops for the Federal armies and on March 3, 1863, Congress passed the Enrollment Act, an outright assertion of national conscription by the central government. This law made able-bodied males between 20 and 45 years of age liable for national military service. The Enrollment Act was not popular, as bloody draft riots in New York demonstrated after Gettysburg. Both the Confederate and the U.S. laws were undemocratic in that they did not apply equally to all individuals. They provided for exemptions that allowed many to escape military service entirely. Comparatively few men were ever drafted into the Federal service, but by stimulating men to volunteer the Enrollment Act had its desired effect.

The principal importance of the Enrollment Act of 1863, however, does not lie in the effect it had on manpower procurement for the Civil War. This measure established firmly the principle that every citizen is obligated to defend the nation and that the Federal government can impose that obligation directly on the citizen without mediation of the states. In addition, the act recognized that the previous system of total reliance on militia and volunteers would not suffice in a modern, total war.

Dimensions of the War

Viewing the war in its broadest context, a historian could fairly conclude that a determined general of the North had bested a legendary general of the South, probably the most brilliant tactician on either side, because the Union could bring to bear a decisive superiority in economic resources and manpower. Lee's mastery of the art of warfare staved off defeat for four long years, but the outcome was never really in doubt. Grant—and Lincoln—held too many high cards. And during the last year of the war, the relations between the Union's Commander in Chief and his General in Chief set an unexcelled example of civil-military co-ordination.

114

In this costly war, the Union Army lost 138,154 men killed in battle. This figure seems large, but it is scarcely half the number—221,374—who died of other causes, principally disease, bringing the total Union dead to 359,528. Men wounded in action numbered 280,040. Figures for the Confederacy are incomplete, but at least 94,000 were killed in battle, 70,000 died of other causes, and some 30,000 died in northern prisons.

With the advent of conscription, mass armies, and long casualty lists, the individual soldier seemed destined to lose his identity and dignity. These were the days before regulation serial numbers and dog tags (although some soldiers made individual tags from coins or scraps of paper). But by the third year of the war various innovations had been introduced to enhance the soldier's lot. Union forces were wearing corps badges which heightened unit identification, *esprit de corps,* and pride in organization. The year 1863 saw the first award of the highest United States decoration, the Medal of Honor. Congress had authorized it on July 12, 1862, and the first medals were given by Secretary Stanton in 1863 to Pvt. Jacob Parrott and five other soldiers. They had demonstrated extraordinary valor in a daring raid behind the Confederate lines near Chattanooga. The Medal of Honor remains the highest honor the United States can bestow upon any individual in the armed services.

Throughout the western world, the nineteenth century, with its many humanitarian movements, evidenced a general improvement in the treatment of the individual soldier, and the U.S. soldier was no exception. The more severe forms of corporal punishment were abolished in the U.S. Army in 1861. Although Civil War medical science was primitive in comparison with that of the twentieth century, an effort was made to extend medical services in the Army beyond the mere treatment of battle wounds. As an auxiliary to the regular medical service, the volunteer U.S. Sanitary Commission fitted out hospital ships and hospital units, provided male and, for the first time in the U.S. Army, female nurses, and furnished clothing and fancier foods than the regular rations. Similarly, the U.S. Christian Commission augmented the efforts of the regimental chaplains and even provided, besides songbooks and Bibles, some coffee bars and reading rooms.

The Civil War forced changes in the traditional policies governing the burial of soldiers. On July 17, 1862, Congress authorized the President to establish national cemeteries "for the soldiers who shall die in the service of the country." While little was done during the war to implement this Congressional action, several battlefield cemeteries—Antietam, Gettysburg, Chattanooga, Stones River, and Knoxville—were set up, ". . . as a final resting place for those who here gave their lives . . ." in lieu of some nameless corner of a forgotten field.

As the largest and longest conflict of the nineteenth century in the western world, save for the Napoleonic struggle, the American Civil War has been argued and analyzed for the more than a hundred years since the fighting stopped. It continues to excite the imagination because it was full of paradox. Old-fashioned, in that infantry attacked in the open in dense formations, it also foreshadowed modern total war. Though not all the ingredients were new, railroads, telegraph communications, steamships, balloons, armor plate, rifled weapons, wire entanglements, the submarine, large-scale photography, and torpedoes—all products of the burgeoning industrial revolution—gave new and awesome dimensions to armed conflict.

INDEX

119